CONTENTS

INTRODUCTION

To a scientist any vitrified mineral or other substance which is naturally or artificially fused, such as obsidian and certain kinds of slag, is glass. But the more usual definition is that given by W. B. Honey in his handbook on the glass collection at the Victoria and Albert Museum, London. 'The material of glass, as the word is commonly understood, is an artificial compound, usually translucent but not necessarily transparent, produced by the fusion of silica in the form of sand, flint or quartz, in a furnace, with the aid of an alkaline flux which may be either potash or soda.'

These are the essential ingredients, but to make a tough and durable glass, small quantities of other substances, such as limestone or chalk or one of the oxides of lead, are in practice required. These last, with the alkali, provide bases for the formation of the complex silicates of which glass is chemically composed. It should be remarked that rock crystal, which glassmakers have constantly striven to imitate, is itself almost pure silica.

Where and how glass was first fashioned into objects has

(left) Beaker of Tuthmosis III, shaped like a lotus flower and with the cartouche of Tuthmosis. About 1450 BC

(right) Map showing chief glassmaking centres in the ancient world

Hamlyn all-colour paperbacks

Derek C. Davis

Glass for Collectors

illustrated by Peter Morter
& Design Bureau

Hamlyn - London
Sun Books - Melbourne

FOREWORD

Collecting glass has a fascination which grows with every new acquisition. Each piece has its own unique qualities of form, decoration and metal, and from an analysis of these comes an increased understanding of the techniques and fashions of this wonderful material. The cross currents of influence from glasshouse to glasshouse and from country to country, and the way in which the craft has gradually evolved through the centuries can be clearly seen.

I sincerely hope that this small volume may prove a useful reference book for those commencing or continuing their study of glass. The historical background which I have outlined should enable the collector to appreciate and assess his collection with greater skill and enjoyment.

The production of this paperback has involved a number of people beside myself whom I should like to mention. My first thanks go to my wife who once again has assisted me so much with my research. I should also like to acknowledge the willing help of the directors and curators of the Pilkington Glass Museum, Lancashire, the Victoria and Albert Museum, London, and the Corning Museum of Glass, New York. Their help in supplying reference material enabled Peter Morter and his excellent team of artists to produce the illustrations which add so much to the overall effect of the book.

Published by The Hamlyn Publishing Group Limited
London · New York · Sydney · Toronto
Hamlyn House, Feltham, Middlesex, England
In association with Sun Books Pty Ltd Melbourne

Copyright © The Hamlyn Publishing Group Limited 1971

ISBN 0 600 00140 7
Phototypeset by Filmtype Services, Scarborough
Colour separations by Schwitter Limited, Zurich
Printed in Holland by Smeets, Weert

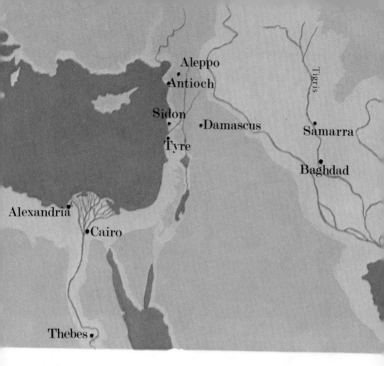

never been discovered, but it is certain that its origins were in western Asia. There is the often-quoted legend of the Phoenician sailors and their chance discovery of glass through the combination of fire, sand from the sea shore and soda from their cargo. But whatever the precise beginnings of glass, there is evidence of glassmaking in Mesopotamia by 2000 BC, although only fragments have survived. The industry began to develop on a large scale in Egypt some 500 years later, and finds there have been much greater. Despite the fragility of this early glass, many objects have survived and pieces are still coming to light. Fresh information on techniques used by early craftsmen, both makers and decorators, can thus be gleaned. During the past few years, glass has greatly increased in popularity and this has been apparent in the growing number of books on the subject and in the high attendance at auction sales, compared with fifteen years ago. The result is, of course, higher prices, but also an increased interest in what has been called the 'eighth wonder of the world'.

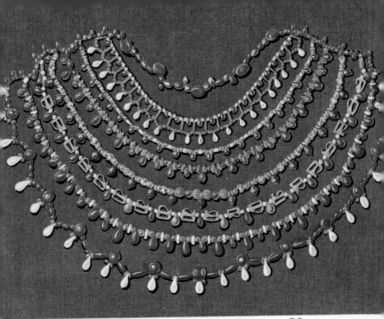

Beads, including eye beads, of first half of 1st century BC

GLASSMAKING IN EGYPT

The unique geographical position of the Nile valley, protected by deserts and sea on three sides and with only a narrow southern border to be defended, enabled its craftsmen to practise the newly-found art of glassmaking in tranquil surroundings. With wide expanses of sand, natron lakes and an abundance of acacia groves, the essential constituents for glass – silica, alkali and fuel – were easily available.

Techniques were at first primitive, for it was not until the Roman era that glassblowing was developed. It seems likely that the glaze which coated early pottery after firing gave Egyptian craftsmen the idea of glass. The glaze could have been chipped off, melted and then reworked to form a vitreous paste. Naturally, small objects were made at first; the earliest were stone or clay beads covered with a blue glaze. Later beads were fashioned in imitation of semi-precious stones and the glass was coloured with powdered turquoise, malachite or lapis lazuli.

The different patterning of the beads provides a clue to

their age. The earliest, dating from around 1550 BC, are striped or spotted. Beads with designs like eyes, zig-zags, chevrons, head-shaped and *millefiori* beads were all later developments. Their smallness and vivid colouring made them ideal for export and many have been found in the Mediterranean region. In Roman times they were exported further afield, reaching Northern Europe, where they acquired a magical significance and were called 'Druids' eggs' or 'Adders' eggs'. Amulets, rings and scarabs, with wings inset with gold and brilliantly coloured glass, were also made. All these ornaments were highly valued and their use was restricted to the royal family.

It was about 1450 BC, during the reign of the pharaoh Amenophis II, that glass vessels began to appear. It was inevitable that these should at first imitate the shapes of contemporary pottery, and typical forms are the *alabastron,* tall and narrow, the *aryballos,* squat and wide-mouthed, the *amphora,* tall, pear-shaped and with a stand, and the *oenochoe,* a jug with a curved handle and flat base. The general size is surprisingly small – between two and six inches in height (five and fifteen centimetres), but the main feature of the decorative style was the use of colour.

Outlined shapes of Egyptian vessels, and *amphoriskos.* About 1450-1350 BC

Methods of manufacture

The gaily-coloured *amphoras* and *alabastrons* of Egypt were used as containers for the perfumes, oils and ointments of court ladies. Glass was still a rare and precious commodity and only the wealthy could afford to own pieces in it. While basic shapes remained the same, a number of methods of manufacture were evolved, as the knowledge and skill of glassworkers increased.

The core method

The first to develop was the core method, in which a core of shaped clay, or of sand wrapped in cloth and tied with string, was fixed to a metal rod and a thread of soft glass was wound round the core until sufficient had been gathered to form the neck and shoulders of the vessel. The glass was then reheated a number of times and marvered (rolled on a marble slab) to smooth and polish it. Forms of decoration, such as the trailing of coloured lines of glass or drops, were applied, and further marvering and light raking with a comb created the typical feathered decoration. Handles and foot-stands were added later with tongs. Finally, the core was removed and when the

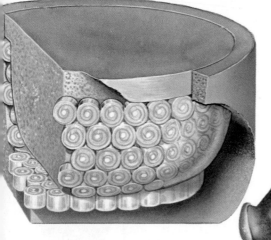

(above) How a *millefiori* bowl was made

(above) Two vases, cast in moulds. 4th-3rd century BC

(below) Bottle in the shape of a fish. 18th dynasty

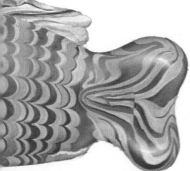

vessel had cooled a trailed rim was formed. The finished glass was reheated after all the imperfections had been ground away, and this gave it a glossy effect. The inside of these vessels is often rough and sometimes there is still sand adhering to the surfaces.

Coloured rods

The ancient Egyptians were masters of *millefiori* (a thousand flowers), and from the fifteenth century BC vessels were formed from coloured rods on a core or base using this complex and attractive technique.

The sections were laid out on a core of the shape of the inside of the glass vessel and loosely fixed together with an adhesive substance. An outer mould was then applied to hold the sections together during heating. The sections were ground smooth after they had been released from the mould. Because of the ductibility of glass, one of its greatest properties, it was possible to draw out the coloured rods to the finest of threads and the pattern introduced into the glass, like the pattern in a stick of peppermint rock, remained unaltered. Bright colours were again popular.

Cutting

Under the Ptolemies (332 BC to 30 BC) Alexandria became the great glassmaking centre of Egypt, and its craftsmen were famous for their fine decorative styles. Apart from the core method and mosaic glass, vessels were also wheel cut entire from a solid block of raw glass and then ground and polished. The main influence in this technique was the art of the stone cutter, and some very beautiful pieces were produced. Simple designs, reflecting the shapes of metalware and pottery of the time, were used, and pure colours were popular, the favourites being sea-green, turquoise and dark blue. The tall narrow-bodied *alabastron* illustrated here is a particularly fine example and shows a rotary movement from within, slight pitting on the surface and many short strain cracks. The latter appeared during the cooling of the glass.

Cutting with a wheel developed during the first century BC and decoration was both intaglio and in relief. The favourite Egyptian motif of lotus flowers is common.

Alabastron, cast in mould.
2nd-1st century BC

Casting

The casting of glass was also a method employed before free-blown glass was invented. It consisted of pouring the molten metal into shaped or carved moulds, and therefore limited the maker to a certain range in his choice of designs. However, this method has been used regularly throughout the history of glassmaking and is very useful for making pieces of the same pattern.

The articles made needed to be open, such as jars and bowls, and the moulds used were either open or two-piece, the former being used for flat-backed objects, and the latter for those of rounded design.

Pâte de verre

One of the most ambitious techniques used was *pâte de verre*, glass ground to a powder and mixed with an adhesive substance so that it could be worked like a clay and conveniently shaped before being fired. However, this never became very popular because great skill was needed to produce an object successfully due to the constant risk of collapse in the kiln when the glass was in a semi-liquid state.

(above) Bowl, cast in mould and with cut petal design. 7th-5th century

(left) Inlaid face of a prince: First half of 1st century

The Egyptian achievement

The Egyptians proved excellent craftsmen, producing an amazing number and variety of objects, both functional and ornamental, despite the fact that they were only pioneers in the art of glassmaking and that technical skill was comparatively slight. Glass differed essentially from contemporary pottery in that it remained a luxury. Obviously the Egyptians loved rich bright colourings and almost all surviving objects are vivid. Perfectly clear colourless glass was not evolved by the skilled craftsmen of Alexandria, and this was a secret which eluded glassmakers for many centuries.

Dating the glass produced prior to the Roman era is not an easy task and needs expert study and archaeological experience, but 500 BC is generally used as a convenient date for the majority of it. The quantity of core-made Egyptian glass which survives does not by any means equal examples of Roman pieces which were made of more durable material. A great number of specimens of early glass have been preserved because of the Eastern custom of burying the dead with their possessions. A number of unusable vessels have been found in burial chambers and this has given rise to the theory that at a later age grave goods were specially manufactured.

Collecting Egyptian glass

Egyptian vessels, mainly produced by the core method, are naturally among the most difficult pieces to find in antique shops or auction rooms, and one article may cost many hundreds of pounds or dollars. They can, however, occasion-

Pharaoh's pectoral in the form of serpents and scarabs, decorated with gold, gemstones and glass paste. 18th dynasty

ally be traced at specialist showrooms and are well worth owning. For a full collection, a typical piece of every variety will need to be represented.

If a traveller abroad has sufficient time while on holiday in the Middle East to search for antique glass, he may have the fortune to find a genuine specimen from Alexandria which will certainly enhance his collection. But the collector must be sure of his knowledge before acquiring any addition in such romantic surroundings.

Palm bowl from Egypt with wheel cutting. 6th-5th century BC

OTHER MEDITERRANEAN GLASSHOUSES

There are few surviving examples of early Syrian and Palestinian glass and these have tended to be overshadowed by the greater quantity and quality of Egyptian pieces. The fact that these early vessels imitate Egyptian styles has been interpreted as evidence that Syrian glass was purely derivative. Egypt gained control of Syria in 1468 BC and glassworks were certainly set up under the aegis of Egyptian craftsmen, but the development of Syrian glassmaking remained erratic because the country lacked the stable conditions which had fostered glassmaking in Egypt. Despite this, however, it is possible that the revolutionary discovery of the technique of glassblowing was made in Syria, and the city of Sidon has the reputation of being its birthplace. The historical facts are uncertain, and both Egypt and Roman Italy have been suggested as the source of the blowing iron.

Syrian glass was not of the quality of Egyptian; it was more fragile and has therefore often survived only in fragments. 'Syrian' is a general name used for much of the glass assigned to the eastern Mediterranean area. Later glass did develop away from Egyptian styles and some original forms were created. After the development of free-blown glass a typical vessel, derived from the tall *amphora,* was the bipartite or tripartite hollow container known as the *balsamarium.* It had horizontal trailed lines of decoration round the body and small looped handles. Like its prototype, the *amphora,* it was an oil or ointment holder.

The relief glasses from Sidon form a separate category; these are long-necked flasks, with rounded bodies often decorated with geometrical designs. Ribbon handles were common. Trademarks and signatures often appeared, such as 'Ennion' or 'Artas Sidon', and these suggest that the glass-makers were Greek or perhaps Hellenized Syrians.

There are innumerable references to glass in the Bible, yet little seems to have survived. Again, Jewish vessels seem to have been made in imitation of Egyptian styles and this makes identification difficult. Glass products were often exported over a wide area and the place where they were found may be very far from where they were manufactured. A few motifs have been established as Jewish in origin and these include the palm-leaf and other Biblical symbols. They have often appeared on the so-called 'Temple' vases. Other Mediterranean places manufacturing glass included Cyprus and Crete, Tripoli and Tunisia. Further east Mesopotamia remained a centre of manufacture. Workers travelled very far and carried the craft of glassmaking to Sicily, Spain, Gaul and the Rhineland.

Bowl, moulded and wheel-cut, from Mesopotamia. First half of 1st century BC

THE ROMAN EMPIRE

The impact of the Roman empire upon the art of glassmaking was to be of vital importance. In 30 BC Egypt was conquered by Augustus and the great glasshouses of Alexandria came under Roman rule. The discovery of the blowing iron dates from around 50 BC and thus the transformation of the glass industry became directly linked to the opening of trade routes within the far-reaching boundaries of the empire and beyond. The Roman skill for accepting and adapting native arts ensured that glassmaking techniques, designs and fashions were dispersed throughout the empire and that new glasshouses were set up far and wide. Although the Romans were in part responsible for the sudden expansion of the glass industry at this time, Italy itself never became one of the chief centres of production. The old glasshouses of Egypt and Syria continued to lead the world.

A certain uniformity of design can be seen in many Roman pieces, arising from the recent technical advances and the speed with which these could now travel over wide distances. But to call all the varied vessels of this era 'Roman' can be misleading as this term refers to the date rather than to the place of manufacture and may cover objects distinctly Egyptian or Syrian in character. The similarity of styles shows that glass found as far apart as the Rhineland and Greece still fits within the mainstream of Roman design – the simple functional shapes in greenish-coloured glass so typical of the Roman period.

Glassmaking has a long tradition as an itinerant trade, its craftsmen moving around from district to district in search of supplies of fuel and the necessary minerals. Simple furnaces could be set up for as long as the workers stayed and easily dismantled when they moved on. The glassblowers were able to sell their own wares, constantly introducing the novelty of their glass to a new market and staying as long as fuel or popularity lasted. By selling their manufactures on the spot the itinerant craftsmen also avoided the problem of transporting a breakable and valuable commodity.

Roman covered cinerary urn, free-blown. 1st century AD

The invention of free-blown glass

The discovery of the blowing iron revolutionized glassmaking techniques and considerably altered the styles of pieces manufactured. A brief description of the new technique may be useful at this point. Whereas formerly glass had been worked around a core, mixed in a prepared mould or ground from a raw block, now a 'gathering' of the materials heated in a crucible in a furnace was picked up at the end of the blowing iron. The craftsmen blew down this, creating a free-blown bubble of molten glass. The ductibility of the molten metal was then exploited by the skill of the workmen to form a variety of shapes. The simplest tools were used for shaping and designing the finished products. There is no definite information concerning the invention of the blowing iron which may have evolved slowly over some years or may have been a chance discovery. The only extant evidence is the sudden appearance of free-blown glass vessels from the year 50 BC onwards.

Previously only small, intricate and very precious articles had been produced in glass, which had been a luxury bought

(above) Helmet-shaped sprinkler from Syria. 3rd century AD

(left) Roman pitcher, in imitation of Greek terracotta wine jar called *askos* and copying mosaic designs. 1st century AD

by the wealthy, but now the increased output from the growing number of sites and the increased ease with which glass could be produced meant that it could reach a wider market. Vessels for everyday life began to appear, and in fact the majority of Roman pieces which survive are functional. These must have been manufactured in large quantities. The blowing iron allowed a much greater range of shapes to be created, including flat designs, such as plates, which were formed by blowing into a mould, an interesting combination of two techniques. Square, globular or tapered bottles, both small and large, were produced, as well as pitchers, urns, bowls and vases. The size of these pieces also increased and the quality of the metal improved.

The invention of glass-blowing did not, however, bring the older techniques of glassmaking to an end. In particular, Alexandria continued to use many styles which had become highly developed. Blowing seemed to be used mainly for functional wares, while cutting, engraving and moulding were used for more expensive items, with decoration.

Roman functional glass

Alexandria, under the government of Rome, still continued to produce luxury glass and a number of elaborate types originated during this period (see page 22). Inevitably surviving pieces are rare. Far more common are the products of the Roman glasshouses in Syria, Gaul and the Rhineland which met the requirements of ordinary households for almost four centuries. The Syrian craftsmen manufactured simple and more thinly blown forms compared with the more advanced techniques of Alexandria. All vessels at this time were tinted or coloured as no decolourizing agent had yet been discovered. Syrian glass tends to have a bluer tone than the pale green of other Roman glass. It was during the second and third centuries AD that the greenish-tinged, almost colourless Roman glass in a wide range of functional shapes began to appear in some quantity.

The earlier the vessel the simpler it usually is, consisting of its basic shape with undecorated mouth and handles. Functional Roman vessels are often closely related to contemporary metalware in their plain, straightforward and somewhat heavy designs. Later, decoration and more elaborate shapes developed. Trailing often appeared around the necks of vessels and it is thought that this may have derived from the string tied round the necks of bottles for the purposes of transportation over distances.

Mould-blown decoration is a frequent feature, including pillar-moulding, or ribbing, which was added while the glass was still soft. Many of these simple articles were blown into one or more moulds to create the required shape and some were decorated with wheel cutting. Vessels were made for holding ointments and cosmetics, pitchers for wine and oil, drinking vessels and table glass for use in the home. There were even glazed windows at this early time. Glass was becoming part of ordinary domestic life.

(top left) Beaker with applied trail decoration. 3rd century AD
(top right) Small bottle with strap handle. 3rd-4th century AD
(centre left) Roman mould-blown bowl. Mid 1st century AD
(bottom) Large cup with folded foot, C-shaped handle and flat rim, in imitation of silver form. 1st century AD

(left) Lycurgus cup, with cut decoration. 4th century AD

(below) Cameo cup from Alexandria. 1st century AD

Roman decorative glass

The cameo technique probably originated in the Alexandrian workshops where increasingly sophisticated grooved, faceted and fluted cutting were all developed. One of the best known and most beautiful techniques was the imitation of cameos. A glass vessel was made in a dark colour, usually deep blue, and was then coated with a layer of opaque white glass. The outer layer was cut, carved and ground away in a design which employed the blue as a background. Great detail and delicacy were possible according to how much of the white layer was removed and there is an amazing amount of anatomical precision and subtle shadowing.

One of the most famous examples of the cameo technique is the Portland Vase, which is now in the British Museum. On this vase the dark ground shows through the thinned portions, giving an effect of depth. For the most intricate work, such as a figure or a tree, hand tools had to be used, small chisels and gravers. The scene depicts the legend of Thetis and Peleus. Thetis, the daughter of the sea goddess Doris, was wooed by both Zeus and Poseidon, but she married the mortal Peleus and became by him the mother of Achilles. The vase dates from the time of the emperor Augustus (27 BC to 14 AD) and, though it has survived the centuries, it was almost destroyed in 1845 by an eccentric when it was on show at the British Museum. Fortunately an exact copy in Wedgwood jasperware existed and this was used as a guide to repair the original vase.

Another style requiring endless patience and a mastery of the art of cutting is the *diatreton*, or cage cup. Here an inner glass cup is decorated with a thin network or cage of glass on the outside, usually forming a geometrical pattern. Clear, greenish-tinged glass is most common although there are a few examples of multi-coloured cage cups. The Lycurgus cup with its more complex figurative decoration and its eerie change of hue from olive green to deep red in changing light is a fine specimen of this unusual technique. The secret of how these cups were made has remained hidden, but it seems most likely that a vessel of thick glass was cast and then a wheel was driven deep into the surface cutting away the unnecessary glass until only the delicate and fragile pattern remained in high relief. A number have been found in the Rhineland and some glass historians believe that the cage cups are German in origin.

The Portland Vase, a mould-blown *amphora* with cameo decoration. 1st century BC or AD

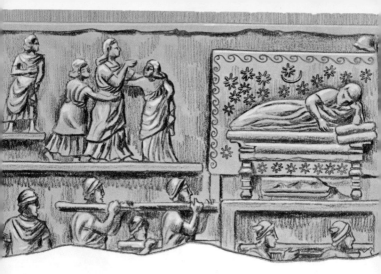

The background is taken from a bas-relief and represents the ritual of a Roman funeral procession

Millefiori and mosaic work also evolved during the early part of the Roman era in Alexandria. The literal meaning of *millefiori* is a 'thousand flowers', and dishes and bowls were made by arranging tiny coloured rods or canes into patterns. It was a technique later to be used for French paperweights in the nineteenth century (see page 122). The technique originated in early Egyptian beads and was a continuing tradition from pre-Roman times. A more general term is mosaic, which was used not only for bowls and jars, but also was incorporated in floors, walls and ceilings of Roman villas.

From the earliest times it was possible to make coloured glass by adding various chemicals to the original minerals which form glass. Sometimes an unusual tint appeared by accident, caused by impurities in the mixture before experiments to eradicate these had been wholly successful. However, some effects of colour in ancient glass, not man-produced, cannot be so easily explained. The practice of burying possessions with the dead continued during the Roman empire and special burial urns and other vessels were produced. Long years of burial caused a partial decay and this in turn produced

Roman bottle with iridescence
found in a tomb

iridescence on the surface of some Roman vessels – a wonderful rainbow-like sheen of colours. In the late nineteenth century this iridescence was to be artificially produced by a number of glass manufacturers in Austria, Bohemia and England.

Collecting Roman glass

There is tremendous scope for the collector in this field of ancient glass because large quantities have survived in good condition. The improvement in the quality of Roman metal is responsible for the many pieces which are now available. The more typical functional glass tends to be sold in lots, groups of two to four, for not over high prices. A good representative piece on its own may cost more. On the other hand a moulded gladiator vase would be very expensive. More rare than the green glass is the pale blue glass of Syria. This has survived in smaller quantities because it was thinner and therefore more subject to decay. It tends to be more expensive than its green counterparts. Roman glass more often than not shows signs of iridescence or of burial in the ground.

Byzantine medallion showing St Christopher, moulded very much in the style of semi-precious stones and dating from 12th to 13th century AD

EARLY CHRISTIAN AND BYZANTINE GLASS

During the second and third centuries AD the Roman empire was struggling to retain its unity against attacks from the North and the East. In 310 AD the official recognition of Christianity took place and in 324 it became the state religion of the empire. The emperor Constantine the Great extended the city of Byzantium in 328, renaming it Constantinople, and transferred his seat of government there two years later.

One unique form of Christian glass, dating from the third and fourth centuries, has been found in the catacombs in Rome. Small glass medallions decorated with gold and showing New Testament scenes or portraits of saints were embedded in the walls of the catacombs and had probably been set there when the plaster was wet. It is thought that they were originally beakers and that the main part was broken off to leave only the base showing. A layer of gold leaf was applied to the glass and then etched with a needle. To complete and preserve the decoration, another disc of glass was laid over the design and fused onto it. Engraved gold leaf decoration was a late Roman development and there are one or two surviving bowls which have very fine gold patterning.

When Constantine moved to Byzantium, it is to be supposed

that a great many craftsmen followed the emperor to his new capital. Little evidence of the Byzantine glasshouses has, however, been found and this makes reconstruction of their history difficult. Rome had for many years been supplied with glass from the glassworks of Alexandria, and Byzantine styles were probably in line with these. When the Roman empire finally fell in 477, trade and industry to the east of the ransacked city would have carried on.

There is a collection of glass in St Mark's Treasury in Venice, which is assigned to Byzantium and was said to have been brought from there when the city was plundered in 1204 by the crusaders and their Venetian allies. It included cups and shallow bowls, cut and mounted as hanging lamps or patens, and there are two coloured bowls cut in relief with hare-like animals. The emphasis in Byzantine decorative styles seems to have been on cutting, for an edict of the emperor Constantine differentiated between *diatretarii*, glasscutters, and *vitriarii*, glassmakers, which indicates that relief decoration was ranked highly. In this it is possible to assume that styles were strongly influenced by fashions at Alexandria and Damascus. The few surviving Byzantine glasses certainly show marked Eastern features in form, colouring and decoration, but these are only a handful from what must have been a large output.

Tall-necked Byzantine bottle following the typical shape of Islamic forms and exhibiting signs of iridescence

EASTERN GLASS

The rise of Islam

In 330 AD Byzantium became the capital of the Roman empire, and with this movement of political power towards the East, there was a corresponding shift in artistic expression. Glass-making declined in the Western empire, and only stereotyped and cruder versions of earlier styles were produced, but the number of glass workshops to the south and east of the Mediterranean increased considerably. Workers moved from one area to another, carrying the traditions and techniques of the industry to new places. Syria, Egypt and Alexandria in particular remained the chief centres, but glass of the period has been found in Trans-Jordan and Palestine, Cyprus and Crete, Persia and Arabia, Mesopotamia and Afghanistan.

The new influence to rise out of the Near East was Mohammedism. The Mohammedan era, which dates from 622 AD when the prophet fled from Mecca to Medina, was marked by continuous wars, as the banner of Islam was carried through successive countries. Under the different caliphates, representing the prophet, the Islamic empire reached out to Syria, Arabia, Egypt and later Persia, Armenia and parts of Africa.

Under Islamic rule the glasshouses continued to manufacture fine glass vessels. The same problems of dating and deciding the place of origin exist because of the wide dissemination of styles. Tall-necked flasks with globular bodies form the main type, but colouring and decoration vary. This basic shape probably stemmed from the Egyptian *alabastron* and *amphora*, and was a favourite of the East. (Roman designs tended to be squarer and wider.) The necks of the flasks and bottles were decorated with trailed threads of glass, and moulded and pincered ornament developed, usually taking the form of geometrical patterns. Glass cutting, closely related to the art of the lapidary, was used by Persian glass craftsmen from the second to the sixth century. The most famous examples of this kind of work are the so-called Hedwig glasses, which are thick-walled vessels of tinted glass, cut with great skill and ingenuity with formalized birds, animals and foliage. This group is named after one glass which was owned by St Hedwig of Silesia. Pale greens, pale blues and amber are most common.

The Luck of Eden Hall, an enamelled Syrian beaker of the late 13th century, owned for many centuries by the Musgrave family and sold to the Victoria and Albert Museum, London, in 1958

Islamic enamelled glass

It is enamelled glass, however, which holds pride of place among the varieties of Islamic glass vessels. Enamel colours are fused onto the glass during firing and in fact the characteristic vivid colouring of enamels only develops after firing. The first, fairly simple examples began to appear in the twelfth century and these are small clear-glass beakers painted with scrollwork and jewelling, or drops of enamel. It is interesting that enamelling on glass developed very shortly after pottery in Persia began to be decorated in the same way, and it shows how different fields of the arts constantly influenced each other. Aleppo and Damascus quickly became centres for enamelling glass.

It was at this time that the crusades were at their height and that small citadels of European power were being held along the eastern edge of the Mediterranean. The rare and beautiful enamelled cups and chalices were prized by the crusaders, and some found their way back to Europe where they were often mounted in precious metals and stones, representing how highly they were valued. The Luck of Eden Hall, still unbroken after many centuries and owned by the Musgrave family until recently, is an exquisite example of such beakers.

As techniques became more sophisticated, more elaborate

Enamelled mosque lamp, probably from Damascus, about 1350. The floral decoration shows the influence of Chinese designs and the lamp is typical of later styles

objects were decorated, and thus evolved the magnificent enamelled mosque lamps. Ornamented in Kufic script with quotations from the Koran or praises to the current caliph, which formed wonderfully intricate and serpentine designs, these are outstanding examples of the fusion of functional and ornamental glass. They serve as lampshades, with the light suspended in a small container inside. The early lamps have three handles from which they were suspended on chains of silver or brass; later lamps have six loop handles. A large number have survived because they were protected by their sacred function and surroundings. In the nineteenth century the majority of the mosque lamps were moved to the Cairo Museum, but there are fine specimens in many museums throughout the world. Vivid reds, blues, greens and gold are the favourite combination of colours, often on a gold-hued glass. The twelfth, thirteenth and fourteenth centuries saw the height of Islamic enamelling, after this there was a decline.

Collecting Islamic glass
Recently two mosque lamps in fairly good condition were sold for £5,000 and £6,800 respectively. At such prices it is clear that the collecting of rare Islamic glass is only within the scope of museums or the very wealthy collector.

Enamelled mosque lamp, from Syria, in the shape of a bell and decorated with geometrical motifs and Arabic inscriptions. The lamp dates from 15th century

(left) Chinese bottle. Mid 18th century

(right) Chinese bowl. Mid 18th century

China
Early glass pieces

The history of glassmaking in China is comparatively brief since glass never assumed the importance which was given to it in Europe, and ceramics remained the supreme Chinese achievement. The Chinese themselves claimed to have been making glass from the fifth century AD, but objects do exist dating from earlier times. These are chiefly glass funeral jewels from the Han dynasty, but some pre-Han beads have been found and have been closely analysed. European beads were imported into China, but the pre-Han beads show interesting variations in design from Western specimens and also an unusually high proportion of the mineral barium. These two characteristics indicate that glass was being produced in China at a date prior to the fifth century AD.

The pieces made during the Han dynasty (206 BC to AD 220) were imitations of the famous Han jades, and possibly were cut from blocks of glass imported from Alexandria. The glass was carved by lapidaries in the same way as they worked precious and semi-precious stones, and was probably regarded as a substitute for jade. During the T'ang dynasty small figures

Tall 18th-century bottle with overlay of red glass elaborately carved with a battle scene, a palace and a background landscape. Probably dating from the reign of the emperor, Ch'ien Lung

of gods, goddesses and animals were cast in moulds and were made as votive offerings. These small glass objects were usually green or colourless and often show signs of iridescence. There appears to be no Chinese blown glass at this time.

The next recorded period for glass made in China is that of the reign of K'ang Hsi (1662-1722) and the majority of surviving examples date from this period or later. The young Manchu emperor, K'ang Hsi, took a lively interest in the cultural development at his court and in 1669 set up a number of factories within the imperial grounds at Pekin, one of which was specifically for producing glass. He was on terms of great friendship with the Jesuit missionary in China, Ferdinand Verbiest, a Netherlander who may well have been able to reveal the secret of Western glassblowing. From this time glass was successfully blown, although it never became a favourite medium for Chinese artists. The early glass from this period exhibits the common flaw of crizzling affecting the surface of the glass and caused by an imbalance in the chemical ingredients used.

Vase in Ku Yuëh
Hsüan style. About
1750

Eighteenth-century Chinese glass

When China eventually made blown-glass vessels, it was natural that these should very much follow the style of porcelain. White opaque vases, closely resembling porcelain, beautifully decorated with coloured enamels, were fashionable, especially in the eighteenth century when both the porcelain and the glass industries prospered under the protection and patronage of the emperor, Ch'ien Lung.

It is possible that artists from the porcelain factories worked on glass as well, and this would explain the similarity and the extreme skill with which the magnificent paintings of bird and flower subjects were executed. In one case, however, it is recorded that the reverse occurred when the emperor was so impressed with the painting of a particular glass enameller called Ku Yuëh Hsüan, which means 'Ancient Moon Pavilion', that he commanded the work to be copied at the imperial porcelain factory.

Other articles were also produced under the rule of Ch'ien Lung. These were intricately-cut belt buckles, snuff boxes and ornamental pieces. The decorative technique used for the snuff bottles was similar to that of the Roman cameo style. A vessel was formed from two layers of different coloured opaque glass; the under layer was often yellow or pale green, and the outer layer a darker colour. The overlay was cut to form a patterning of foliage, flowers, dragons, birds and figures, and often Chinese symbols were incorporated in the design. The majority of pieces made in China from 1736 to 1795 are two-colour bowls, vases and bottles, and, like the earlier Han glass, these have a jewel-like quality. Other attractive pieces are the self-colour sugar bowls in clear blues, greens, reds and pinks. These are recognizable through their characteristic hard texture and shiny surface.

Collecting Chinese glass

Some collectors decide to collect Chinese glass within a certain colour range, such as a group of white with green or white with pink bowls. Yellow remains the rarest Chinese colour in glass. Self-colour bowls are always popular and taller pieces with coloured edges and sometimes with decoration fall into the semi-rare category of salerooms.

EUROPEAN GLASS IN THE MIDDLE AGES

North European glass dating from the period AD 500 to 1400 is rare, and surviving pieces show no sign of technical advances. One important reason for the scarcity of European glass vessels from this time was the prohibition by the Church on burying worldly goods with the dead. At death the Christian soul abandoned all material possessions, which were obstacles between it and eternal life. This important means of preserving pottery and glass was, therefore, lost to the world, and from now on pieces only survived through chance.

The metal of the North European vessels is heavier and cruder than that of earlier Roman pieces, showing flaws and bubbles often, and the colour is usually deep green. Some of the earliest objects are drinking horns, which were made in the same shape as the ivory oliphants carved from animals' horns. They have no foot and were either supported on a stand or handed back to a servant when they had been drained. The top was usually decorated with lines of threading,

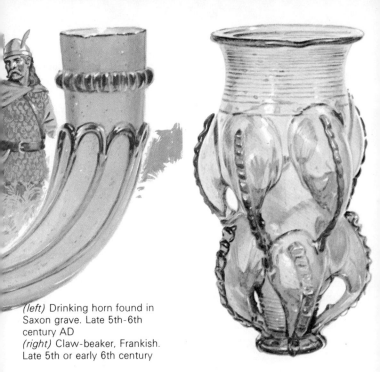

(left) Drinking horn found in Saxon grave. Late 5th-6th century AD
(right) Claw-beaker, Frankish. Late 5th or early 6th century

and the sides were often fluted. A later and more complex development was the claw-beaker, which retained the horn shape but was given a rather clumsy foot and the sides were decorated with hooked bosses of trailed glass.

Other simple pots, bottles and beakers were made, often with trailed decoration, and the most common colours were green, yellow and brown. It was in Gaul and along the Rhine valley that the majority of glass vessels were made. Glasshouses were established in forests for the sake of the fuel supply, and produced *Waldglas*, or forest glass, a form of potash glass. There are a few recorded instances of glass workers in England, such as Laurence Vitrearius.

Collecting medieval European glass

Glass from this period is not common, and technically it never reaches a high standard. Collectors who wish to have a representative collection may find that gaps occur at this point.

THE RISE OF VENICE

Despite the importance of Venice as one of the outstanding glass centres of the world, very little is definitely known about the founding of the city itself or the early development of the glass industry there. It seems likely that refugees from Aquileia, the settlement sixty miles east of Venice, driven out by the army of Attila the Hun, fled to the islands of the Venetian lagoon in 452 and established themselves there. Unsuitable though the site was for extensive building, a city gradually arose. Venice was ideally situated as a trading centre at the threshold to the East, and its commercial enterprises flourished. Soon, the republic controlled trade with the East, and its growing navy consolidated its power and its trading interests.

During the crusades, the city supplied the European warriors with the necessities and the luxuries of life, and in return it extended its territorial possessions, gaining control of Crete and a host of seaports along the eastern coast of the Mediterranean. A long period of struggle followed between Venice

The Fairfax Cup, a Venetian enamelled cup. Late 15th century

and the rival mercantile port of Genoa. In 1204 Venice formed part of the force which attacked and captured Constantinople, carrying off considerable treasures as a consequence. With Constantinople subdued and the prominence of Venice secured, the threat from Genoa receded, and in 1381 the Genoese fleet was devastated by the republic.

The origins of glassmaking in Venice are traced back to the fall of Constantinople, for it is thought that Byzantine glassworkers came back to Venice and there set up a glasshouse. The earliest glass objects produced seem to have been mosaics, used to decorate the domes of churches in northern Italy, and small medicinal bottles and flasks. Very few of these first glass pieces have survived, owing to the brittle nature of the metal then produced, and historians have to rely mainly on documentary evidence. Most of the early information about Venetian glassmaking has been preserved in Benedictine manuscripts dating from this period, and the Order was clearly closely associated with the industry through the roles of patron and customer.

Map showing Venice and later glassmaking centres in Europe

Enamelled marriage goblet in opaque white glass. Late 15th century

The development of Venetian glass

In 1279 Venice began to export glass to the surrounding states of Italy and by the end of the fourteenth century Venetian glass was being sent to the Netherlands and England. Little unfortunately survives from this period and export pieces were probably fairly simple bottles, jugs and flasks. In 1290 a glassmakers' guild was formed which was divided into categories of those who made vessels, glass in mass, spectacles, looking glasses, large and small beads, and which also included general dealers in glass. Surviving records show that the Venetian glassmakers were held in high esteem and that glassmaking was a respected craft.

With the expansion of the Venetian glass industry a number of regulations were issued by the Grand Council of Venice to control the organization of workmen, working hours and even techniques of the trade. The glassworkers were forbidden to leave the republic and heavy penalties were imposed on those who broke this rule. The danger of fire caused the government of 1291 to transfer the glassworks to the

island of Murano where they have remained to this day. However, in 1292 the order was amended and small glassworks were permitted in Venice, for making such objects as beads, as long as the glasshouses were fifteen paces away from any houses.

After years of perseverance and experiment, the Muranese glassmakers produced their unique metal, *cristallo*, so called because it resembled the clarity of rock crystal. The discovery in 1463 has been attributed to the Muranese glassmaking family Berovieri, which is still manufacturing glass in Venice today. The new *cristallo* glass superseded the earlier *communi* metal which was inferior in quality.

Muranese metal was soda glass, the soda being obtained from marine plants, such as *barilla*, which were abundant in this mineral, and the sand from nearby rivers. The resulting glass was light, often yellow or brown in tint, highly plastic while molten and capable of being blown into elaborate and fantastic shapes. The clarity of the metal, the greatest improvement of the new *cristallo* glass, was caused by the addition of manganese, as a decolourizing agent.

Clear-glass Venetian goblet, decorated with colourful enamelling, ribbed foot and knops. Early 16th century

Decoration of Venetian glass
Enamelling

Islamic enamelled glass must have often passed through the hands of enterprising Venetian traders, and yet Venetian enamelling seems to have been a separate development. It may be that the art reached Murano through the Byzantine glassworkers who were brought from Constantinople in 1204. The style of Venetian enamelling, the forms of vessels to which it was applied and the enamel mixture itself all differed from Islamic materials and this seems to point to an independent evolution.

The enamel colours, prepared from finely-ground coloured glass, contained some sort of flux, such as borax, to aid fusion, and were mixed with an oil to make the substance fluid. The enamel was then applied like paint and fired in a kiln to fix it. Only through many years of use did the colour sometimes become chipped or rubbed.

The first Muranese enamelled vessels appeared around the end of the fifteenth century and are in the style of the Italian Renaissance. They were usually goblets, dishes known as *tazze*, and beakers, all in coloured glass. The most common colour was a deep cobalt blue, although green and white both occur. A number of these early specimens were marriage gifts and are decorated with suitable mythological scenes, such as Venus in a chariot drawn by doves, or medallion portraits of the bride and bridegroom. One famous piece of coloured glass is the Fairfax cup, now in the Victoria and Albert Museum, London, which is in turquoise glass.

With the development of *cristallo* glass, clear-glass pieces were also decorated with enamel. The enamelling was now designed to offset the clarity of the metal and the almost classical quality of the forms. Jewelling, scale patterns and rosettes, all formed from beads of enamel, and thin lines of gilding were the most common motifs. Scrollwork and grotesques and occasionally heraldic devices appear. As glassmaking improved thinner glass vessels were blown and these were likely to become misshapen if reheated to fire the enamelling. This was one of the reasons why enamelling in Venice passed out of fashion towards the middle of the sixteenth century.

Clear-glass reliquary, decorated with blue glass foot and cross, gilding and enamelling. Late 15th century

Clear glass and blue trailing

The Venetian *cristallo* glass was hailed as such an achievement chiefly because of the contrast it presented with the kind of glass produced in the centuries immediately preceding its development. Though not without its own greyish or yellowish tint, it did approach transparency and brilliance. The thinner it was blown, the clearer the metal appeared.

In early pieces the mantle, or underside, of a *tazza* was joined to the foot by a glass ring called a *nodus*, from the Latin word for knot. The Dutch word *knoop* or *knop* became the current term in England. This glass ring became a globular knop, or when it was flattened, a collar. Later Venetian drinking glasses had conical-shaped bowls with a lower and only slightly domed foot. The knops grew in number to form the baluster stem.

Not content with the graceful and delicate forms of these thinly-blown glasses, Muranese glassworkers began to produce innumerable variations on the theme. The stems sprouted curling and complex wings, sometimes in the shape of lions, dragons, or sea horses. These fantastic shapes were of course only possible because of the extreme pliability of the soda glass while soft. Mixtures of styles also occurred, such as *latticino* with crackle glass (see page 49) on the same goblet. In the sixteenth century mascerons, or lion masks, became fashionable on knops, and were often powdered with gold.

The most common combination with clear glass, however, was trailing or threading in blue glass. A goblet of *cristallo* glass usually has wings of blue glass, forming a figure of eight or twisting spirals. This flamboyant design was often repeated on a smaller scale surmounting the cover of the drinking glass.

As stems became more complex, the foot became heavier to balance the extra weight of decoration which it was carrying.

Clear-glass vessels were also decorated with gilding, which was either fired on like enamel or cold painted. Some Venetian dishes have survived with only dull smears where the gold decoration used to be. Gilding was usually in the form of fine lines, emphasizing edges, or of scale and beading patterns.

Imitations of semi-precious stones

Calcedonio, glass resembling semi-precious stones, such as jasper, agate and chalcedony was a revival of an Alexandrian style. Aventurine was made by adding oxidized copper. This fashion developed late in the fifteenth century and continued for some time, although large numbers of these pieces were never produced. *Millefiori* vessels were also made in the fifteenth century, and like *calcedonio*, were imitations of the Roman patterning.

(right) Ampulla in *calcedonio* glass with gilded Arabic script. Early 16th century. The shape imitates metal forms

(left) Clear-glass plate, decorated with bands of gilding, *latticino* and diamond-point engraving. Mid 16th century

Diamond-point engraving

Although diamond-point engraving occurs occasionally on Muranese glass it was not ideally suited to soda glass because the metal was thin and brittle. Engraving endangered the life of such a glass too seriously to be often used. German potash glass, which was considerably heavier, was well adapted to the technique, and so it was in the German and Dutch glass-making centres that engraving became a fully developed art (see pages 61 and 74). There are examples of Venetian engraving, however. The cutting is always a light and delicate scratching of the surface, with no delving deep into the metal. Patterns tend to consist of detailed twining foliage and flowers. The *tazza* with its wide surface area was the most suitable object for engraving and therefore the most commonly used. The decoration forms a wide band round the edge of the dish contrasting pleasantly with the clear glass of the rest of the piece.

Lattimo glass

The opaque white glass, known in Murano as *lattimo* and as *Milchglas* in Germany, made its appearance fairly early in Venice. Dating from around 1500 there are *lattimo* goblets enamelled in the decorative styles mentioned earlier (see page 43). The density of the white could vary from a deep white to a semi-transparent colour, and it was an effective background for the vivid enamels. Attractive though this pairing was, *lattimo* involved a concealing of the intrinsic qualities of glass and a disguising of it as something else. At this time, the opaque white glass did not therefore achieve any real popularity.

Towards the end of the seventeenth century there was a revival of interest in it, when its resemblance to porcelain was noticed. Chinese porcelain was being exported to Europe where it was prized almost as highly as jewels. Various kings and princes set up experimental porcelain works and employed chemists and potters to search for the secrets of porcelain manufacture. In the meantime, opaque white glass was exploited as a substitute for porcelain, and it was often blown and decorated so skilfully that only an expert would have detected that it was glass. Exactly the same kind of decorative motifs were used as were employed on porcelain – delicate bunches of flowers, fruit, birds, and later figures and scenes, sometimes in *chinoiserie* styles. Two families became particularly associated with work in this field – the Miottis, active from 1731 to 1747, and the Bertolinis. At first the painting was in polychrome enamel, but later black, sepia and red monochrome became fashionable for executing scenes of Venice and landscapes. These possess a greater air of sophistication. Plates, such as the one illustrated, would have been decorative rather than functional.

Opaque white glass plate, painted in red with a view of San Giorgio Maggiore, Venice, probably at the Miotti workshop. About 1741

Latticino glass

A direct development from *lattimo* glass was the delightful and original *latticino* design, in which fine threads of opaque white glass and clear glass alternated. At first patterns were comparatively simple, forming a network design, and the glass was known as *vitro di trina*. Later a more complex patterning developed, which had a lacy effect and was called *vitro a reticelli*. A series of straight rods or canes of white glass were placed vertically at regular intervals along the inside wall of a mould. A gather of clear glass was blown into the mould, fusing with the canes. If the vessel was twisted, the white canes would also twist, and the pattern would be formed. For greater complexity the gather could be blown into a second mould containing white canes and a criss-cross design would result.

This style appeared usually on wineglasses, ewers and *tazze* of comparatively simple form, and would be used for the feet and covers as well as for the body or bowl of the object. The delicacy and skill of the work maintained a high standard and *latticino* must be counted as one of Venice's supreme achievements in glass. There are occasional examples with coloured threads but these are not common, and the original pristine design of white with clear glass held its position undisputed.

Crackle glass

A rare type of glass is the Venetian crackle, or ice, glass. The surface of this glass is covered with thousands of tiny cracks, creating an irregular effect. Two methods have been suggested for making this type of glass, first, that when a glass vessel had been blown and while it was still hot, it was plunged briefly into cold water, thus causing the minute hair-line cracks to appear all over the surface. Alternatively, the piece could have been marvered on a bed of splintered glass while it was still soft, and then reheated so that the slivers of broken glass would fuse to the body. Whatever the technique used, crackle glass again reveals the Venetian love of strangeness and variety.

Covered goblet vase in *latticino*. Late 16th century

Mirrors, lighting and later developments

In 1500 Venetian craftsmen developed a new technique for making mirror glass – the broad process. This replaced the crown technique (see page 120). The Venetians were famous for their fine mirror glass and virtually controlled the trade until about the middle of the seventeenth century, when some of the market passed into the hands of French factories. Venetian mirrors were beautifully decorated with ornate metal frames. Often octagonal in shape, the frame was usually wheel-engraved, gilded or set with decorative coloured glass in the form of flowers or semi-precious stones.

Chandeliers formed another branch of the industry and provided another opportunity for the imagination of the Muranese craftsmen. Splendid glass chandeliers of pincered and moulded glass, with flowers of brightly coloured glass, were typical. Ornament was the keynote.

During the eighteenth century Venice had to compete against the porcelain factories and the popularity of their products. As a result the Muranese glasshouses began to develop along rather different lines. Baskets of glass fruit, vases of flowers, miniature gardens, birdcages, Moorish figures and animals were all produced in vivid colours. Always bright and gay, these pieces nevertheless represent the insecurity of the Venetian glass industry.

Collecting Venetian glass

Venetian glass is difficult to find and prices vary considerably. Anything gilded or enamelled in particular is very expensive.

Glass novelty in the shape of a basket holding fruit. Late 18th century

Bowls with enamel decoration and coloured glass bases are sometimes included in sales of mixed glass, but there are crude versions about, and the fineness of both the gilding and the metal need to be carefully assessed.

Portable mirror with ornate gilded frame. Late 17th century

FAÇON DE VENISE

Although Venice stands pre-eminent in the history of glass-making, both for its great technical advances and for its development of so many original designs, it was not responsible for the spread of this increased knowledge through the rest of Europe. The Glassworkers' Guild of Murano jealously guarded its secrets, and severe restrictions were imposed on its workers by the Venetian government. Glass craftsmen were not allowed to leave Venice, and betrayal of the guild secrets to a rival glassworks carried the death penalty. Even the export of discarded glass fragments, known as cullet, from the workshop yards was punished, since this would have allowed an analysis of the formula of the famous Venetian *cristallo* glass. Yet despite these penalties, workers did escape from Murano to places such as L'Altare, Padua, Treviso, Vicentia in Italy and further afield to Flanders, Bohemia and England.

Glassworks were set up in all of these places. L'Altare itself, perhaps the most important centre outside Venice, did not restrict the freedom of movement of its workers from one place to another, and so the new techniques eventually spread throughout Europe. At first, obviously, the vessels produced were very close to the Venetian prototypes. This was because the craftsmen of Murano were at the height of their creative powers, and the glass produced at their factories was far in advance of other independent attempts. Also, so many of the workers in these different places were Venetian in origin that they must have continued the styles of work which they knew so well. These glasses have since been given the name of *façon de Venise*. So faithful are they in style and spirit to the Venetian originals that it is often virtually impossible to be certain of the provenance of the glasses. The export of Venetian glass inspired craftsmen throughout Europe.

Amongst the most active factories which produced *façon de Venise* glass were those established in the Netherlands. As early as 1541, Italian craftsmen had set up furnaces there. In 1569 there was a glasshouse in Liège, and further works are recorded as being in operation in Amsterdam (see page 60).

Dutch *façon de Venise* engraved goblet. 17th century

The styles of façon de Venise

There were Italian glass-makers working in the Netherlands, Spain, France, Germany, Denmark, Sweden and England, and a variety of *façon de Venise* styles developed from the middle of the sixteenth century to the end of the seventeenth century. Perhaps the most famous centres were Liège, Antwerp, Hall, Nuremberg and London. Differentiation between Venetian and Venetian-style vessels remains difficult and the only general comments that can be made are that *façon de Venise* glasses tend to be often in a slightly darker or straw-coloured metal. The proportions of drinking glasses also are sometimes lacking in the grace and balance of Muranese goblets. A large number of Netherlandish glasses were of the complicated winged-stem type, either in a figure of eight or looped formation, and decorated with coloured imprisoned threading and pincered ornaments. Small scrolls, crests and openwork decoration of all kinds were included on the stems.

Other vessels from the same factories were made with multi-knopped stems, sometimes with as many as five on

Winged and engraved Dutch goblet. Late 17th century

the same stem, and each was surmounted by a collar, so that knops and collars alternated. These winged glasses with comparatively small bowls, long baluster stems and wide feet to weight the glass were an extreme version of a once simple style. The Dutch decorators often included their own speciality of diamond-point engraving and stippling on the bowls of *façon de Venise* goblets (see page 62). In the same way German *façon de Venise* combined rich coloured glass bowls and feet with winged stems in clear glass. Some tall tankards were made in the *latticino* pattern at Liège, but these never quite attained the quality and intricacy of Venetian designs. These vessels often had pewter covers and metal mountings.

Another style based on L'Altare glass also developed and this was distinguished by gadrooning, applied work and finials. Again motifs and materials were interchangeable and many different combinations were tried. Early in the seventeenth century Renaissance styles were gradually superseded by Baroque designs. This led to even more fanciful ornamentation of glass than before.

Winged goblet with trailing, Dutch or Belgian. 17th century

Two-handled pitcher, known as a *jarrito*, from Andalusia, with blue glass decoration. 17th-18th century

GLASSMAKING IN SPAIN

The development of Spanish glass

In spite of the fact that records seem to show that glassmaking was in progress continuously from the time of the occupation of Spain by the Romans, nothing distinctive, either in pattern or material, appeared until the fifteenth and sixteenth centuries. Some glass historians suggest that the craft almost disappeared in the seventh century, and only survived through the conquest of southern Spain by the Moors and the impetus which their new culture gave to all branches of the arts. A further important influence during the early years was the import of Mediterranean glass. Vessels from Damascus, in particular, were extremely popular; sometimes rare pieces became heirlooms, handed down from generation to generation. Islamic-style pieces survive and it is difficult to decide whether these were made in Spain or further afield.

In 1455 a guild of glassblowers was formed in Barcelona and from then on the craft gradually advanced. Regulations to protect Spanish cities, where glass was being made, from the risk of fire were introduced and strictly enforced. In the sixteenth century glasshouses in Andalusia, Castile and Catalonia were producing glass in greater quantities. Northern glasshouses tended to follow in the wake of Murano, Catalonia and Barcelona being most prominent among these, while southern furnaces developed forms which were still in line with the Moorish designs. The metal produced in Catalonia could not equal Muranese glass; it was a smoky colour and was known as *fumé* glass. The Venetian decorative styles of enamelling, *lattimo* and trailing were all employed and the inevitable Spanish *façon de Venise* was produced.

The factory set up at La Granja de San Ildefonso, near Madrid, in the eighteenth century produced fine glass vessels in the style of European glass of the period. Bohemian crystal glass, in particular, was imitated, and a Spanish version of the Baroque developed. The La Granja glasshouse is renowned for the splendid chandeliers it manufactured, composed of polygons of clear glass. Other pieces were decorated with faceted flowers and foliage, with gilding and enamelling.

Wine jug with swan neck, strap handle, ribs on the body and spiral trailing around the rim. Mid 18th century

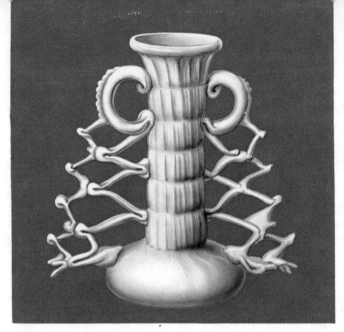

Glass in southern Spain

It was through the influence of Moorish styles, and especially of the Hispano-Moresque pottery of south-east Spain, that the most original of Spanish glass designs evolved. Glassmaking never flourished in Spain as it did in such countries as Bohemia or England, but nevertheless it did create some unique forms. These vessels have retained their own local names, the *almorratxa* or *almorrata,* the *cántaro* or *cantir,* and the *porron*. Other pieces were the *botijo*, a squat bottle, and the *jarrito*, a small mug.

The *almorratxa* was a holy-water sprinkler, of complex form, with four hollow tubes from which the water was poured, a tapering body and pedestal base. Varieties of this vessel were produced in Catalonia in the seventeenth and eighteenth centuries. The *cántaro* was made as a container for drinking water. It had a globular body on a tall foot, a large ring handle on top, often surmounted by a stork, cockerel or other bird, with one narrow spout on one side and a wider one on the other. It could be used as a communal drinking vessel, supplying a thin stream of liquid when held above the

(left) Candlestick in opaque white glass, showing Islamic influence. 17th-18th century

(below) Cántaro, from 18th century, in clear glass with blue glass trailing and *latticino* decoration. The Moorish influence is strong

mouth and without coming into contact with the lips. The *porron* was also used as a drinking vessel, but only possessed one long spout jutting out from a flask-shaped body.

Spanish metal tends to be heavy, with flaws and often greenish-tinted in colour. The influence of both Venetian and Moorish styles led to a great deal of decoration being used. *Latticino*, trailing with applied turquoise glass and inside threading often appeared, while the bodies were frequently wrythen-moulded, or spiral moulded, in true Venetian manner. Pincered ornament, which was executed on the soft glass with red-hot pincers, regularly decorates the many handles and the bodies of the vessels in crests, ruffs and ripples. Stringing, or threads of glass applied externally, and prunting of a particularly Spanish type were also used. Small glass rings were hung on handles or from hooks.

Collecting Spanish glass

Very little is available to the collector outside Spain, and pieces, when purchased, are usually chosen to complete a collection, rather than for their own intrinsic beauty.

Dutch still life showing *façon de Venise* goblet and *Stangenglas*

GLASSMAKING IN THE NETHERLANDS

In 1549 Antwerp granted a licence to an Italian glassworker, allowing him to manufacture Venetian-style glass. Naturally, the glass produced was at first directly derived from Murano designs, but later it developed towards the freer elaboration of Venetian styles, known as *façon de Venise*. Liège glassworks also flourished, well situated on the banks of the river Meuse, and supplied with raw materials from the seaport of Rotterdam and other nearby cities.

The metal of the Netherlands was of two kinds, the Venetian soda glass and the German *Waldglas*. The Dutch never developed an individual distinctive style or metal, although they became highly skilled as decorators. The soda glass was used for ornamental pieces in the spirit of Venetian designs, while the *Waldglas* appeared in the form of the typically Germanic *Römer*. This was a drinking glass with a tall rounded bowl, a wide stem decorated with prunts and a domed foot. Dutch *Römer* were lighter than the German glasses, but equally popular, for they figure importantly in many seventeenth-century Dutch paintings of still life or indoor scenes with sumptuously laden tables.

Drinking glasses were made with complicated coloured twist-coiled stems, mostly with covers and sometimes with octagonally-shaped bowls. A tall slender glass, narrowing at the foot, called a flute glass, was another favourite, but unfortunately few have survived.

Engraving on glass

The decoration for which the Netherlands were justly most famous was diamond-point engraving. In the seventeenth century this type of ornamentation ceased to be common in Venice or Germany, but it continued long after in the Netherlands and there reached its peak. Although in the history of glassmaking fewer individual names of craftsmen have been known than in most other branches of the arts, fortunately many of the finest Dutch engravers signed and dated a fair proportion of the drinking vessels they decorated. Diamond-point engraving was a favourite pastime for many Dutch people with artistic inclinations. The pieces decorated were usually single items, presentation glasses to celebrate a christening, wedding or other important event. The result is a surprising variety and originality.

(right) Römer, enamelled in sepia with a scene showing Mercury finding the young Bacchus. Late 17th century

Diamond-point engraving

In the early seventeenth century Dutch diamond-point engraving tended to be light and delicate, with an emphasis on linear designs. The artist, with a diamond point in its holder, drew freehand on the glass, possibly using as a rough guide a pattern already marked in some way. The engraving did not cut deeply and therefore was suitable for thin-walled wine-glasses. The most renowned artist of this time was Anna Roemers Visscher, 1583-1651, whose work was never surpassed. Flowers, insects and plants were frequent motifs in her decoration and were probably drawn from the natural history books popular at that period. Her sister, Maria Tesselschade, was also an expert engraver, with a similar style.

During the last half of the seventeenth century wheel engraving, which was the forte of German glass decorators, influenced Dutch styles. A stronger contrast between light and dark superseded the earlier and more sensitive engraving. Portrait glasses and fine calligraphic work became popular.

Wheel engraving

The introduction of lead glass from England in the eighteenth century, with its qualities of strength and brilliance, transformed Dutch methods of engraving. The German-derived wheel engraving, which bit more deeply into the glass, could now be safely employed. Jacob Sang is perhaps best known for this kind of work and a number of glasses signed by him have survived from the years 1752 to 1762. Scrollwork and formalized foliage decorate the glasses, and some goblets are engraved with Dutch shipping scenes or heraldic devices. At the end of the century etching on glass was developed.

Stippling

Frans Greenwood, 1680-1761, is the name most commonly associated with the development of diamond-point stippling, although A. Schuman and Anna Roemers Visscher made use of the technique occasionally. A diamond was set in a handle and then gently tapped with a hammer to produce a design by a series of dots, very close in appearance to screen printing in photography today. Shadows and highlights could be rendered more easily, the untouched polished areas of the glass contrasting with the stippled parts. Decoration was exceedingly delicate and of great charm. Signed pieces by Greenwood date from between 1722 and 1755, and many of the glasses have Newcastle baluster stems. A later and skilled exponent of stippling was David Wolff, 1732-1798, who worked mostly on glasses with faceted stems and signed and dated a number of them. A number of unsigned glasses have also been attributed to him on the grounds of style.

(left) Flute glass with diamond-point engraving. Mid 17th century

(right) Goblet with diamond-point engraving, dated 1686

Römer with cup bowl, raspberry prunts and a milled ring at the top of the stem. The foot is made up of threads of glass. About 1655

Trick glasses

A separate development from the weird and wonderful prunted beakers of the Netherlands and Germany, but connected in spirit, were trick glasses.

The craftsmen of the Netherlands were famous for their trick glasses, flasks in the shape of ships with a network of glass to form the sail, drinking straws in the shape of horses, and every variety of animal or fish. These are now rare for their extraordinary forms make them especially fragile.

Dragons, horses and all kinds of fantastic animals were used to create the elaborate and complex stems of Venetian goblets and *façon de Venise* glasses of the sixteenth and seventeenth centuries. Several other countries at one time and another were producing glass novelties for use or purely as toys. Three of the most notable were Spain, where hats, shoes, oil lamps and baskets of woven glass rods were produced for sale at fairs, England, where the hats were worn and the walking sticks carried in processions, and France, where the beautiful little glass figures from Nevers were so popular (see page 120). The ductility of glass enabled it to be blown and shaped in the complicated formations of trick glasses, and allowed glassmakers of many ages to exercise their imagination and their sense of humour.

Collecting Dutch glass

Although glass from the Netherlands is available in England and North America from time to time, it needs a great deal of searching for and is not widespread. It is safest to buy only well-known authenticated pieces of glass which occasionally appear in salerooms. A fine example of Dutch *façon de Venise* could command a high price. Most expensive is glass dating from the seventeenth and eighteenth centuries.

The main problem is the difficulty of distinguishing definitely between Venetian and Dutch glasses because of the similarity in styles and metal. Obviously, a far larger selection of Dutch glass exists in the Netherlands and the enthusiastic collector would be well advised to search there for fine examples of the various types of glass made in the Netherlands.

Trick glass with a drinking straw in the form of a stag. 17th-18th century. This was a common form of novelty glass

GERMAN AND BOHEMIAN GLASS

The medieval vessels made of *Waldglas,* or forest glass, in Germany have already been mentioned (see page 37). This thick greenish-coloured metal continued to be manufactured for some centuries and the early glasses were robust and primitive in form. *Nuppenbecher* and *Rüsselbecher,* claw-beakers and trunk-beakers, were the main types produced and were decorated with blobs of molten glass shaped like thorns, claws or hooks. The most extreme representative of this form was the *Krautstrunk,* or cabbage-stalk glass, a tall glass the sides of which bristle with thorny prunts so that it closely resembles its name.

During the thirteenth and fourteenth centuries a number of factories were established in well-wooded regions in Germany and Bohemia, such as the Seine-Rhine area, and the industry began to expand, especially in Bohemia. The influence of Venice was clear, and glasshouses set up in Hall, Innsbruck, Nuremberg and Munich in the sixteenth century were on the direct trading route for glass with Venice. Many

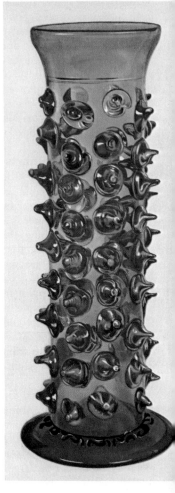

Stangenglas in *Waldglas* and decorated with prunts, probably from the Rhineland. Early 16th century

Map showing glassmaking areas in Germany, Bohemia and the
Netherlands from the Middle Ages to the 19th century

of the early jars and cups survived because sacred relics were
buried in them under the altars of various churches. The pre-
Christian custom of burying possessions with the deceased
had come to an end with the dominance of the Church throughout Europe.

The green colour of German glass was caused by the
presence of iron and other chemicals in the metal, and many
craftsmen experimented to find a clear and flawless glass.
About the same time that Ravenscroft succeeded in making
English glass of lead which was to excel all its rivals (see page
86), some success was similarly achieved in Bohemia. Potash
replaced soda in the mixture of materials, and chalk was also
included. The result was the production of clear-glass thick-
walled beakers and goblets which could be carved to a greater
depth than previously. Wheel engraving became the chief
means of decorating the new Bohemian crystal glass.

Types of glasses

The *Römer* was one of the most popular Germanic forms, remaining in use from the Middle Ages until the nineteenth century. From the simple medieval beaker-like vessel developed a more elaborate form in which the top became larger and bowl-shaped, set on a wide stem decorated with prunts, and standing on a domed foot made from threads of glass. From the mid sixteenth century, button or looped prunts appeared on the barrel-shaped beakers. One clergyman described them in 1564, 'Nowadays one applies buttons, prunts and rings to the glasses to make them sturdier. Thus they can be held more easily in the hands of drunken and clumsy people. This is the reason why these rigid and bumpy vessels are favoured by so many.' The prunts of the seventeenth century became flatter, and the very attractive raspberry prunt was evolved, in which a series of tiny drops of glass were grouped to form a circular prunt.

The *Humpen* was a plain straight-sided glass with a slightly flared foot. It was the form most commonly used for enamelling since it presented a wide and smooth expanse of glass to the painter. Variations were the *Reichsadlerhumpen* and the *Kurfürstenhumpen,* so-called because of their decoration (see page 70). Similar to the *Humpen* was the *Willkommen* which could only be differentiated by its inscription. It was a greeting glass, made and kept especially to hold drinks for guests. In the same family of glasses was the *Passglas,* which was decorated with horizontal lines of enamel or threads of glass. This glass was passed from hand to hand in the beer-cellar and each drinker was supposed to take the amount of liquid marked by the line on the glass. Finally, there was the *Stangenglas,* a tall thin version of the *Humpen,* which was decorated with lines of glass and stood on a hollow foot.

Simple beakers were common, and because the feet were usually applied it is possible to detect the join in the glass. Flasks, bottles and goblets were also made in some quantities. An unusual flask developed in the seventeenth century. This was the *Guttrolf* or *Angster*. Its globular base is decorated with moulded flutes and an applied foot, while the neck, which is of a twisted pattern, leans aslant. It was probably used as a sprinkler or slow-pouring vessel.

Beaker or thumb glass in *Waldglas,* with cavities sunk into the glass where fingers and thumb could be inserted. 16th-17th century

Beaker in *Waldglas,* decorated with looped prunts and with a notched trailed ring below the rim. Probably 16th century.

German enamelled glass

Enamel is a paint which is fused onto the surface of glass at a temperature lower than that at which glass melts. An alternative, cold painting, is not fused but is held on the surface with an adhesive. The former method became very popular with the German artists, as it was far more lasting than cold painting which tended to rub off too easily. Clear brilliant colours were used, often with a dense white, on a greenish-tinged glass.

The earliest German enamelled glasses, dating from the late sixteenth century, were made in the style of Venetian pieces, and are often virtually indistinguishable from these. There is evidence that some glasses were made in Venetian metal and painted by German artists, which makes identification even more difficult. Dated examples, however, tend to be German in origin as this was a Germanic custom. Family crestings and coats of arms were popular devices and these give further help in establishing the provenance of particular glasses.

Most formal and elaborate of all the designs common on the enamelled glass of this period is that on the splendid *Reichsadlerhumpen* (Imperial eagle tankards). Blazoned around these

(far left) Armorial beaker, dated 1671, *(left)* enamelled Household beaker, dated 1696, and *(below) Reichsadlerhumpen,* dated 1594

tall *Humpen* is the double-headed eagle of the Holy Roman Empire with its wings outspread and hung with the fifty-six shields of the electors, landgraves, margraves, counts and other landholders who comprised the empire. At the neck of the eagle is an orb, although this is sometimes replaced by a crucifix. A variation on the theme are the *Kurfürstenhumpen* (Electors' tankards) which display the emperor seated on his throne, flanked by the seven electors. Inscriptions in praise of the emperor are common.

Another unique design is the *Ochsenkopf* (ox-head) glass, which shows the fir-covered mountain of that name in the Fichtelgebirge region, an important glass-making area. More common motifs are the hunting, riding, or drinking scenes, all filled with homely and slightly naive people. Whole families are illustrated encircling *Humpen,* and there are numerous guild glasses showing craftsmen at work. Allegorical themes, such as the Ages of Man, political events, Biblical scenes, saints and apostles, together with many other vignettes of everyday life and thought in Germany, cover the glasses.

Hausmaler and their work

The eighteenth century brought a change in the styles of decorating glass which considerably affected the production of enamelled glass. The success of the Meissen factory and the demand for porcelain led to a substitute porcelain being developed, known as *Milchglas*. Enamelled glass had arisen out of, and had been very much involved with, the life of middle class merchants and craftsmen. The more sophisticated decoration of wheel engraving which reached its heights during the eighteenth century was preferred by the courts and as a result enamelling declined both in quality and quantity. It remained mainly as a peasant art.

A separate tradition of decoration developed in Germany in the seventeenth century and continued during the eighteenth century. This was the work done by *Hausmaler,* self-employed artists who worked at home or in their own workshops and who bought undecorated glass and porcelain and enamelled it in their own individual styles. The decoration was usually highly sophisticated.

Johann Schaper, 1621-1670, was the first well-known *Hausmaler*. Originally he was a painter of stained glass and some of the techniques required for this medium can be

Covered goblet enamelled by Johann Schaper in *Schwarzlot* with portraits of the emperor Leopold I and his wife Margaret. A realistic fly is enamelled on the bottom. About 1665

detected in his work on glass vessels. Born in Hamburg in 1621, he worked in Nuremberg from 1665. He mainly painted in *Schwarzlot,* black enamel, and *en grisaille,* grey, with touches of red and gold. One technique which he used very effectively for fine detail was scratching through the black enamel with a needle. In contrast he sometimes added realistic humorous touches, such as a convincing fly on the bottom of a drinking vessel, which came into sight when the contents had been drained. Schaper signed and dated a number of pieces. Johann Faber painted in the style of Schaper, usually landscapes, flowers and figures. There were a number of other *Hausmaler* working at this time, some are known by name, others remain anonymous.

In the eighteenth century Daniel Preussler and his son, Ignaz, Silesian glasscutters, became renowned for their enamelling on porcelain. They usually worked in *Schwarzlot, en grisaille* and in red and purple monochrome. They also decorated glass. *Chinoiserie* was popular and was often used alongside the more conventional Baroque motifs of scrollwork, foliage and shells. Callot figures, after the work of the French etcher Jacques Callot, who invented a special kind of grotesque figure, were also used.

Tumbler, from Nuremberg, enamelled in red by a *Hausmaler* and showing four Callot figures. About 1720

Wheel engraving in Germany and Bohemia

It was at the court of the emperor Rudolph II in Prague that wheel engraving on glass was revived at the end of the sixteenth century. Wheel engraving had been used in ancient times as a means of decorating glass, but it had never equalled the skill and delicacy of gem-cutting. The technique began with a design drawn on to the plain surface of a glass. The vessel was then pressed against a rapidly rotating wheel of stone or copper, which traced the outline of the design; the actual cutting was done with the help of abrasives, such as emery powder. Wheels of different sizes determined the width and depth of the cut.

The emperor Rudolph was an enthusiastic patron of the arts and gathered around him at his court a number of lapidaries. Foremost among these was Caspar Lehmann, 1570-1622, a stone-cutter from Ulzen, who produced in 1605 his only signed beaker decorated with wheel engraving. Portraits, scenes and floral and plant motifs were popular, and were often copied from contemporary engravings. Georg Schwanhardt, Lehmann's pupil, continued the art of wheel engraving and sometimes included diamond-point engraving in his designs as well. Although Lehmann remained pre-eminent, Prague attracted a number of other outstanding glasscutters, including the Schindler family, Friedrich Killinger and Hermann Schwinger. During Rudolph's reign the art spread to Bohemia, Saxony, Thuringia and to Munich and Nuremberg.

Around 1680, at the time when George Ravenscroft produced glass of lead in England, Bohemian craftsmen perfected their own crystal glass. Iron-free potash replaced soda and chalk was added to result in a strong and brilliant glass. The fragility of the earlier metal had to a certain extent limited wheel engraving and had prevented any deep cutting. But now the wheel could be driven deep into the glass to create dramatic contrasts of light and shadow. The glass could be cast in more varied shapes with the stem and foot as part of the piece and not added later.

Nuremberg-type goblets were very fashionable, the stems ornamented with a variety of knops and collars, or flattened knops, and the bowls cut with scrollwork, classical scenes, medallions and historical events. The later designs are more

Two engraved goblets from Potsdam and Augsburg. About 1720

formal than the early decorations, with elaborate details engraved with amazing and meticulous precision. Intaglio work was common, when the design appeared below the surface of the glass, rather than standing out in relief. Both high and low relief work developed and tended to be specialities of the Berlin factory.

German coloured glass

During the 1680s experiments to develop a perfectly clear potash glass were nearing success. Johann Kunckel, 1630-1703, a chemist, was put in charge of the glasshouse at Potsdam owned by Frederick William, the Elector of Brandenburg, in 1679. In that year he published his book *Ars Vitraria Experimentalis*. The glass produced at Potsdam was at first affected

Covered beaker from Potsdam in Kunckel's ruby glass. The engraved Bacchanalian scene was executed by Gottfried Spiller. About 1700

by clouding, owing to too much alkali in the mixture, which could lead to decay in the surface of the glass, known in England as crizzling. By 1689 he had published a second edition of his book and had invented a formula which combated decay by introducing chalk into the batch.

But Kunckel's most famous and noteworthy achievement was the development of a rich ruby-red glass, the colour of red currants. This was produced by using gold chloride as a colouring agent. He learnt the secret from another chemist called Andreas Cassius. The red glass soon became fashionable and was often mounted with finely chased metal. Some of the finest examples were deeply and expertly engraved by well-known artists, such as Gottfried Spiller who decorated the covered goblet illustrated here, with a scene from classical mythology. The red glass remained a speciality of Potsdam, the technique involving care with the cooling to ensure that the distinctive colouring developed.

Red was not the only colour created during these years, blue, purple and green also appeared. It is interesting to note, however, that blue glass from Potsdam is usually thick, which suggests that difficulty was experienced in using cobalt oxide for colouring thinly-blown glass. The Potsdam house also developed *Milchglas,* or *Porcellein-glas* as it was sometimes called. This opaque white glass was produced by Kunckel in competition with the porcelain from Meissen.

Kunckel's experimental glasshouse was burnt down shortly after 1688 and a few years later he decided to leave Potsdam, due to the large number of intrigues which had sprung up against him. After travelling in Sweden, he was ennobled as Kunckel von Löwenstern. He died there in 1703.

During the eighteenth and nineteenth centuries German glassmakers developed a wide range of colourings. Glass in imitation of precious stones again became the vogue. *Hyalith,* an agate-like glass of either black or red, is one example which was developed in Bohemia. A later invention was *Lithyalin* which Friedrich Egermann, 1777-1864, produced. Nineteenth-century pieces are very much in line with English and American styles, glass overlaid with various colours, or covered with a coloured flash being common (see page 133).

Gilding and Zwischengoldgläser

In about 1730 in Bohemia one of the most exquisite decorative processes was revived, which attained lasting success. This was a technique known as *Zwischengoldglas,* gold between glass. A specially shaped glass was made and the outside surface was decorated with gold leaf, or sometimes with silver leaf. Another glass was then fitted around this to protect the design and the two were cemented together and the edge gilded. The double-walled vessel was usually finished by cutting the outer surface with narrow flutes from top to

Zwischengoldglas beaker decorated with hunting scene in fine detail, about 1730

bottom. Decoration was not just restricted to gold or silver leaf, for straw, paper and other materials were all employed from time to time. Johann Mildner, *d.* 1808, was a well-known craftsman who used this technique. He employed gold, silver and red lacquer.

The most common shape was the small straight-sided beaker, and designs took the form of hunting, commemmorative and household scenes, all with a dainty fairy-tale quality. The decoration was always delicate, and the detail was sometimes scratched with the point of a needle. Fired gilding and oil gilding were also used by German decorators, usually in the form of bands or edgings to enamelled scenes or around the rims of glasses. This style was a direct descendant of gilding applied to glass during the Roman era. Gold leaf in a delicate tracery of leaves and flowers decorated some fine Roman bowls. The gold medallions of the early Christian period found in the catacombs in Rome were also encased in glass in the manner of *Zwischengoldgläser* (see page 26).

Collecting German glass

It is possible to obtain a good representative collection of glass, according to the pocket of the collector. As in most cases the earliest specimens are the most difficult to find and are the most expensive. The German *Waldglas,* even though the metal is of inferior quality, is very rare in England and prices are difficult to estimate. Three of the rarest categories of glass and therefore some of the most sought after, are the sixteenth-century glasses, such as *Passgläser,* the enamelled glasses and *Schwarzlot* examples. For those interested in collecting enamelled glass, more care is needed to guard against copies than with almost any other kind of glass. A large number of copies do exist and these can be distinguished by a metal which is almost too perfect and by enamelling even more vivid than on original *Humpen.*

Schwarzlot glasses are not frequently available, and usually are only for sale when a collection is auctioned. If the collector is interested in highly coloured glass, the period 1820 to 1840 offers a wide scope in the form of brightly coloured or gilded beakers. If a glass enthusiast can travel to Austria, for example, he will find such glasses can be bought in their hundreds.

GLASSMAKING IN ENGLAND

Early glasshouses

Until 1676 England had not figured importantly in the glassmaking world; it had contented itself with producing fairly simple wares for the home market and in being a customer for the fine Venetian glasses of those times. The Romans brought the art of glassmaking to England and there is evidence of glassworks dating from the occupation. Isolated glasshouses must have continued after the Roman legions left England, perhaps producing glass in the style of the German *Waldglas,* but no identification of definite English types has been possible. In 674 Benedict Bishop founded a monastery at Wearmouth and he brought over Frankish craftsmen to make glass for the windows of the church. This remains the first recorded instance of glassmaking in England.

Better known is Laurence Vitrearius (meaning glassmaker),

a Norman who set up his glasshouse near Chiddingfold in the Surrey-Sussex Weald in 1226. He must have been successful in his venture, for in 1240 Laurence supplied window glass for use in Westminster Abbey. His son, William le Verir (also glassmaker), continued his father's craft, specializing in window glass, but probably also manufacturing small glass flasks and bottles. Other French glassmaking families, the Schurterres and the Peytowes (names which were possibly corruptions of Chartres and Poitou), joined Laurence's descendants in Chiddingfold, and the glasshouses quietly prospered.

The items made in these early days of experiment were crudely-fashioned bottles, tapering or cylindrical in shape, antecedents of the modern medicine phials, and of a similar green to the German *Waldglas*. Only fragments of this early English glass have been excavated, but these are sufficient evidence to show how active the industry was. Glass was also produced in Colchester, York and Bristol, but the Chiddingfold district remained the most important area well into sixteenth century.

Two important glassmakers

England owed the establishment of all its early glasshouses to foreign craftsmen. The next influential figure to appear on the English scene was Jean Carré, a businessman who had already successfully run glassworks in both Arras and Antwerp. He reached England in 1570 and settled in the Weald, bringing with him a group of Lorraine glassworkers. This invasion was not welcomed by those already established in the Weald, and after the death of Carré in 1572 the new glassmakers travelled about England, carrying the secrets of their craft with them and setting up fresh furnaces wherever forests were plentiful, or, later, coal supplies. The Lorraine names of de Hennezel, de Thietry, du Thisac and du Houx were soon anglicized in a variety of forms, such as Henzey, Tittery, Hoe and Tyzack, and these names crop up commonly in glassmaking records for the next few centuries.

Carré also brought to England seven Venetians, among them Giacomo Verzelini, and put them to work at the Crutched Friars' glasshouse in London. When Carré died, Verzelini took

(above) Making crown glass and *(left)* early glassmakers at work

over the direction of the furnace. It flourished for two years until in 1575 it was destroyed by fire, the billets of wood stored for the furnaces increasing the size of the blaze. There is a suspicion of arson, since Verzelini's ambition to produce English glass in the style of Venetian wares challenged the livelihood of the merchants selling Venetian glass in London. In spite of this great loss, Verzelini applied for a patent to manufacture glass and rebuilt the glasshouse in Broad Street.

On the 15th December, 1575, he was granted a patent by Elizabeth I for a period of twenty-one years provided that he taught the art of glassmaking to the queen's 'natural subjects'. Protected also by a prohibition on imports, Verzelini's business thrived for the seventeen years he managed it. His contribution to English glassmaking was of great importance, for although only a small number of surviving vessels, all engraved with diamond-point decoration except for one gilded goblet, have been ascribed to him, and these are still in the fragile soda glass, he had opened the way for an established industry and for the expansion of the following years.

DISCORDIA FRANGIMUR

The years after Verzelini

There were still four years of Verzelini's monopoly left when
he retired and sold his business to Sir Jerome Bowes, a retired
soldier turned businessman. During the years that followed
the glass industry in England fell into the hands of men who
wished to exploit its commercial advantages. One of the first
changes was the experimental use of coal instead of wood, for
supplies of woodfuel were fast dwindling. In 1615 the
government forbade the use of wood entirely for the glass and
iron industries. Glassmakers had hesitated to use coal before
through fear of it contaminating the clarity of the glass, but
technical advances overcame the problem. Sir William
Slingsby devised a coal furnace specially for glassmaking and
Thomas Percival evolved the crown covered pot which
reduced pollution to a minimum. Bowes, with no experience
of glassmaking, was behindhand with such innovations and
after paying a high price for his licence to manufacture glass
for twelve years, he died in 1616 with his business in an
insecure position.

Once again an attempt was made to acquire the much-sought-
after patent and Sir Robert Mansell with a group of other
entrepreneurs was granted the licence. However, he soon
bought out his partners and his licence was extended to cover
the manufacture of every kind of glass at Verzelini's glass-

house in Broad Street. By 1623 he was in charge of the entire glass industry, owning large numbers of glasshouses in different parts of the country. Mansell was primarily an administrator, and he organized the industry on a firmly commercial basis, with coal supplied from the Newcastle mines and a proper system of transport for carrying the raw materials to the various furnaces.

In 1664 the Glass Sellers' Company was founded, comprising both manufacturers and merchants, and this was to have an important effect upon the techniques and the artistic standards of the industry. The company at first imported Muranese glass, but then began to send designs to be made to order in Murano. The best known of these are John Greene's, which have been preserved in the British Museum. John Greene and Michael Measey, two glass dealers, sent their designs to Venice between the years 1667 and 1672. Dissatisfaction with the way the designs were being carried out and the large number of breakages in transit led to an increasing determination to find an English substitute for the Venetian soda glass.

George Ravenscroft and the discovery of glass of lead

The Civil War in England had a disrupting effect upon the glass industry, but once the Restoration had taken place and order was re-established, it began to make progress again. George Villiers, Duke of Buckingham, was granted a patent to manufacture glass and although his interest in his glasshouses was spasmodic, the industry did advance under his control.

In 1673 George Ravenscroft, an experimental chemist, built a glasshouse in the Savoy and petitioned Charles II for a patent. He stated that he was working in 'a particular sort of Christalline glass resembling Rock Crystall, not formerly exercised or used in our Kingdom'. After a temporary agreement with the Glass Sellers' Company, in 1674 he was engaged by the company as its official glassmaker at its furnace in Henley-on-Thames. It was as a result of samples of his glass of lead that the company accepted his services and in return he received financial backing and the assistance of trained workmen and equipment.

The glass still exhibited crizzling, however, one of the recurring problems of the trade, in which some time after completion the metal developed innumerable hair-line cracks caused by an imbalance in the mixture of materials.

Ravenscroft had been a trader and shipowner, and had spent some time in Venice where it is likely that his interest in glass began. His experiments with oxide of lead created a metal of great clarity and toughness, but the problem of crizzling still haunted him for some time. By 1676 this seems to have been partially at least solved, for the company granted him the right to use a raven's head, taken from his own coat of arms, as his seal on the glass he produced. This was to indicate clear glass, free from crizzling, and in 1677 the success of his experiments was publicly announced.

Lead had the effect of making the metal more pliable when soft, but also heavier and more brilliant. Lead glass had already been described in *L'Arte Vetraria* by A. Neri, which was translated into English by Christopher Merret in 1662. But Ravenscroft was the first to bring it successfully into being. It was also known as flint glass, because it was once thought that calcined flints were used. Two kinds of metal were produced from the 1680s and these were known as single-flint glass, which was thin, and double-flint glass, which was thick.

In 1681 Ravenscroft died and his place was taken by his assistant, Hawley Bishopp. It was probably due to the efforts of the lesser known man that glass of lead was perfected, finally freeing it from the last impurities which had darkened the tint of the glass. By 1700 'glass of lead' dominated the market.

(right) Ravenscroft goblet, with raspberry prunts. About 1676

(below) The Buggin bowl from the Ravenscroft glasshouse. 1676

English eighteenth-century glass

Just when English glassmakers were able to begin producing glass of high quality in earnest the government passed an act levying a tax of 20 per cent on glass of lead and glass plate, and one shilling a dozen on common glass bottles for five years. This act of 1695 was to raise money for the French wars. There was a strong outcry and three years later it was repealed, and the industry then entered the golden age of the eighteenth century.

The new English glass surpassed all other metals manufactured at that time. Although the Venetian influence was manifest in earlier examples, such as the short ale glasses, the glass of lead was heavier than soda glass and was unmistakeably superior in colour and brilliance. It is the drinking glasses which most clearly represent the art of the English glass craftsmen of the eighteenth century. Relying on classical proportions and the new reflective qualities of the metal, these glasses are in themselves small works of art. Large numbers were produced in varying styles, and they can only be classified according to stem groups.

First period 1685-1730

Heavy balusters, 1685-1710, or first period drinking glasses as they were called, developed from the short stemmed seventeenth-century ale glass with its tapering bowl and wrythen, or spiralled, moulded decoration and winged stem. Heavy balusters appeared in both wine and goblet form. They were of particularly fine size and metal and imitated the baluster columns of silver candlesticks and the turned work done by cabinetmakers of this period.

Knops are the solid shapes, usually globular, which form the stem, the number of the most important being twelve. The earliest and simplest type dating from the later seventeenth century was the true baluster, usually inverted. The usual names for knops in order of rarity and earliness, are true baluster, cone or egg-shaped, acorn, mushroom, drop, annulated or triple-ring and ball. The last is often used in combination with other knops. The knop originated on Venetian *tazze* (see page 44) and developed over a number of years in a number of interesting styles and shapes.

Light balusters, dating from 1724 onwards, are most attractive glasses, made on a smaller scale than the heavy balusters, and with the stems composed of a series of minor knops of different kinds, though rarely with any of the very early ones listed above. At this time collars, or flattened knops, were incorporated into stem designs. These light balusters are also known as Newcastle glasses as the majority were manufactured there. Many expert engravers from the Netherlands frequently chose to engrave these graceful glasses.

(top right) English baluster goblet. 1690
(bottom left) English ale glass. 1685-90
(bottom right) English baluster goblet. 1710

Second period 1730-1740

Plain stems with bowl and foot variations proved most popular with customer and glassmaker alike. Most examples were two-piece glasses with the bowl drawn into the stem, in contrast with the more complex earlier productions of balusters, which were made in sections.

Plain stem glasses were made in large quantities to meet the heavy demands for both tavern and home use, and they were cheap to replace. This style was so generally used that it

(left) Wineglass with plain stem and gilded bowl. About 1730

(right) Wineglass with plain stem, drawn trumpet bowl and ridged foot. About 1730

overlapped other stem designs which followed during the remainder of the eighteenth century.

Because of their simplicity and inexpensiveness they were sold in dozens by weight, rather than as individual glasses, which is the reason why they are the easiest to find at the present time. In spite of these very definite changes in design, the fine quality, colour, and general robustness of English glass did not alter.

Although these plain stem glasses are often the most ordinary in any of the stem groups, some which are engraved with unusual subjects, such as those connected with the Jacobite rising of 1715, can be placed amongst the rarest. These were engraved with verses from the National Anthem together with a crown, or a number of other motifs, and are known as 'Amen' glasses (see pages 101 and 102).

Quite often small features in drinking glasses made them attractive, such as a 'tear' or 'bead' of air which appeared in the early stems or bases of the bowls before the intentional 'drawing out' of the air spirals, along the whole length of the stems after about 1740. These air 'tears' were sometimes large enough to make a hollow stem. Bowl shapes include all the well-known types which continued throughout the century. A rare feature in this phase, mostly connected with cordial glasses, was the domed foot. The width of the stems can vary considerably, from very slender to quite heavy.

Continental fashions had most effect upon English glasses from about 1720 to 1735, and this can be seen in the stems of drinking vessels, sweetmeats, tapersticks, candlesticks and *tazze,* made in England during these years. Instead of a series of knops, or plain stems, the design was often moulded with a slight spiral effect. Other stems were moulded in the shape of four pedestals. It has been claimed that this particular style was introduced by George I, the first English king of Hanoverian descent, and it is known that there was a glasshouse in Laucus in Hanover in 1701, where he could have seen this style. The rarest of all examples in this group have a moulded inscription on the pedestal stem: 'God Save King George'. This style probably lasted until the middle of the eighteenth century, and remains popular with collectors today. The pedestal style is rarer than the Silesian stem.

Third period 1740-1755

Glassmakers were not allowed to remain exempt from the heavy burdens of taxation, and in 1745, just after air-twist stems came into fashion, a new act was passed taxing the raw materials of glass. This proved to be of such advantage to the state that it was doubled and later quadrupled, and was not repealed until 1845. No less than eighteen further acts had in the meantime supplemented or varied the original duties.

At least two excise officers were quartered in every glassworks, whose duty it was to register the total weight of glass melted. They had to be notified before any pot was heated or filled, before any *lehr* (the annealing oven, variously spelt *lehr*, *leer* or *lear*) was heated or closed, and before any glassware was removed from the *lehr*.

From air beads, bubbles and tears came new ideas for decorating the stems of wineglasses. Some change was necessary in order to adapt to the new laws controlling the weight of glasses. It was realized that these trapped air bubbles could be utilized to enhance the beauty of the glasses and would fit in with the new designs for lighter glasses. The craftsman dented the surface of the metal he was working with a blunt metal tool. The depression was then covered with a second layer of glass and the air trapped inside expanded with the heat, forming a spherical bubble. This became

Dram glass with drawn trumpet bowl, colour twist stem and firing foot. About 1760

Copy of 18th-century candlestick with air spiral stem

elongated into a pear shape when the stem was drawn out. In the experimental stages mainly drawn bowl (two-piece) glasses were made and at first the air threads were imperfectly worked, either not reaching the base of the bowl or of the stem.

As the designs grew more complex and daring, they also began to be produced in varying combinations and therefore most glasses fall into categories, such as single series, double, triple or compound. The twists are known as mercurial, corkscrew, coil and silver rope, among others. Knops of different sorts were introduced to enhance the effect, while the full range of bowl designs continued, the most common being the trumpet and the bell, and the rarest, as with all eighteenth-century glass, the double ogee. The folded foot became less and less common as the century progressed.

Wineglass with 'hammered' round funnel bowl. About 1745

(left) Wineglass with a Beilby enamelled pastoral scene. About 1760

(right) Wineglass with moulded bowl. About 1760

Fourth period 1755-1780

The greatest change in the stems of drinking glasses came through the substitution of white opaque glass threads for air spirals. These, on account of their density, showed up even more clearly in contrast to the clear glass of the bowls and feet.

By about 1755, the technique of using air threads had been perfected, and it was not surprising that this further idea of inserting opaque glass materialized.

As the proficiency of the work increased, the English glassmakers were able to evolve many different arrangements of corkscrew, simple coils and lace-like twists. Sometimes, as in the previous stems, double series and triple series patterns were inserted in the same stem. Some of these were so thin that they presented a gauze-like appearance when covered with clear glass.

Over a hundred varying combinations of twists and spirals have been recorded.

(left) Wineglass with Beilby enamelling and opaque twist stem. About 1760

(right) Dram glass with colour twist stem. About 1760

Varieties of twist are multiple spirals, gauze spirals, cork-screws (sometimes edged with a single spiral), tape, lace and cotton twists. The three-piece construction was nearly always used for these glasses, although quite a number have come on the market with drawn bowls during recent years.

Those with knopped stems have been classified into different sections as follows: knopped glasses with single series twist, knopped glasses with a double series twist, unknopped glasses with a single series twist, unknopped glasses with a double series twist.

Opaque stemmed glasses were still being made with folded feet, but this feature had become even rarer. Wheel engraving was widely used with an extensive range of subjects, including landscapes, floral motifs, and domestic scenes. The superb enamel technique of the Beilby family (see page 102) is almost always associated with these glasses, since they worked on wineglasses and goblets about 1755-1770. Gilding appears occasionally, but less often than enamelling in colours.

Fifth period 1770-1800

Cut or faceted stems became popular in the late eighteenth century. Having explored the possibilities of decorating the inside of stems, the glassmakers turned to yet another way of ornamenting wineglasses—this time by cutting, or faceting as it is more usually called. This change was probably influenced by the introduction of the enamel tax in 1777, which led to a reduction in the use of enamel. Designs decorated the whole length of the stem, and included shallow flat diamonds, hexagons, and vertical flutes, or slice cutting.

As early as 1740 Thomas Betts, polisher and grinder of mirrors, advertised his 'various sorts of cut glass ware', but cutting became generally fashionable in late eighteenth-century designs. The festoon ornament on the bowls of glasses was inspired by the decorative style of the Adam brothers. Glasses of this period were generally light in weight and many designs were cut or engraved on the bowls. An interesting group can be collected to show the different designs on the stems, including elongated diamonds, elongated

Sweetmeat with flat cut geometric cutting. About 1780

Wineglass with cup-shaped bowl and faceted stem. About 1780

hollowed diamonds, hexagons, close-scale facets, and grooving, vertical flutes, small diamonds and other variations. Vertical fluting continued into the nineteenth century on all decanters and wineglasses. Sometimes, the fluting was carried into the base of the bowl forming an attractive 'rose' design when the drinker looks into the bowl.

The usual designs were floral and bird subjects, but more complicated landscape and sporting scenes also occur. Some of the glasses from this period were decorated by the best Dutch engravers, Wolff and Greenwood, and are wonderful examples of their superb stippling technique.

Knops in this stem group were not common. The usual bowl shapes were the round funnel, ogee, drawn tapering and lipped cup—the rarest being once more, the double ogee.

The feet of some glasses were made with double the normal thickness and these were sometimes cut, with occasional scalloped edges. Some had domed and folded feet but these are now difficult to find. In all these five main periods of drinking glasses, other variations can sometimes be found which do not fall within these recorded groups.

Wineglass with rounded bowl and faceted stem. About 1790

Wineglass with double ogee bowl and faceted stem. About 1780

Variations in formations

So far we have considered the main phases of drinking glasses. There were a number of variations from about 1730 in stems, and variations in bowls and feet also occurred.

Twists of many kinds decorated the stems of drinking glasses. Incised twists were made by making close wrythen, or spiral, grooves on the outside of the stem in the style of Venetian glass. They are now quite rare, especially when combined with knops. These glasses were subsidiary to the air twists and appeared about 1740 to 1760. Mixed twists were made containing both air and opaque spirals from 1755 to 1770, and they form a small but important group for the collector. Most were made with bell-shaped bowls, but other designs included the long round funnel, short round funnel, ogee and rectangular bell bowls. It was a highly specialized group, as the style required great skill, but almost all examples which come to light are finely made.

About 1760 experiments to introduce coloured threads into the stem, with either air or opaque spirals, were successful. The combination of coloured threads with opaque twists remained the most rare, however. Transparent colour-twist threads in blue, pink or turquoise, combined with air spirals were the earliest made in this group. Later opaque white

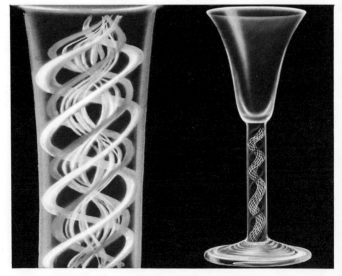

twists were combined with colour. The shades in order of rarity are yellow, green, tartan (a combination of blue, green and red), red with white and blue, red with pink, dark and light blue. A small minority were made with air, opaque and coloured spirals.

Bowl shapes were made according to certain standard patterns throughout the eighteenth century, irrespective of period or stem pattern. They are known as – tapering or funnel, round funnel, bell, rectangular bell or waisted bucket, bucket and lipped bucket, ogee (an architectural term denoting a long S-shaped curve), double ogee, ovoid, trumpet, rounded or cup-shaped, thistle, hexagonal and octagonal.

The folded foot added strength to the base of a glass and prevented easy damage. During the formation of the foot, the metal was extended slightly beyond the narrow diameter and turned underneath to form a 'fold' or double layer of glass. Sometimes this strengthening technique was also applied to the rims of bowls, vases or jugs during the early period.

(left) Detail of colour twist stem
(right) Wineglass with air and colour twist stem
(left) Wineglass with incised twist stem and honeycomb bowl
(right) Kings Lynn tumbler

Decoration on glass

Gilding was not common among English craftsmen and most pieces which survive are drinking glasses. The most popular designs were hops and barley motifs on ale glasses or occasionally vine leaves on wineglasses and, very rarely, on ale-shaped bowls which were probably for champagne. On coloured glass simulated wine and spirit labels in gilding made a pleasing contrast with the blue, green and amethyst of decanters. The corresponding initial of the name was on the stopper. Other designs were urns, figures and landscape scenes, often attributed to James Giles, a famous decorator of glass and porcelain, who also supplemented the decoration with intricate networks of floral designs and birds.

Engraving in England could not match Dutch craftsmanship. The best quality Newcastle glasses were imported by the Dutch for their engravers to work upon (see page 62). No English engravers have been recorded, but fine examples of English work have been found, the best examples being the fine Jacobite glasses engraved with the verses of the National

(left) Armorial goblet signed Beilby with double series opaque-twist stem. About 1760

(centre) Champagne glass with gilding and double series opaque-twist stem. About 1760

(right) Sunderland Bridge goblet. About 1798

Anthem. Decorative motifs include coats of arms and family crests, portraits and emblems, scenes of gambling, with the hollow base incorporating dice, pictures of transport, commerce and trade, historical events, naval occasions, such as Lord Nelson's flagship and his funeral car to commemorate his death. Most of these subjects were engraved on large tumblers, goblets and wineglasses and are now difficult to come by. The engraving is not always contemporaneous with the glass itself.

One of the favourite subjects for collectors are the Jacobite glasses, in memory of the '45 rebellion and the events leading up to the defeat of Prince Charles Edward at Culloden in 1746. A common theme is a rose with one or two buds. The rose has been interpreted as England with the buds as Charles's father, James, and Charles himself. Other emblems are the oak-leaf, star, thistle, compass, which is extremely rare, and the portrait of the prince, in fine detail, with one of a number of Latin mottoes. Most frequent is 'Fiat' (may it be so), but there is also 'Audentior ibo' (I will go more boldly) and 'Reverescit'

(left) Beilby goblet with white enamelling, in the form of vine leaves and fruit, and opaque-twist stem. About 1760
(right) 'Amen' Jacobite glass with drawn trumpet bowl and air-twist stem. Diamond-engraved with the National Anthem. About 1715

and 'Redeat' etc., all expressing the hope of a Jacobite victory. These glasses were made for the loyal supporters of Charles Edward so that they could toast the success of the movement in the various Jacobite clubs.

Enamelling was at its peak in England during the years 1755 to 1770, when the Beilby family was in operation. William Beilby senior, 1705-1765, was born in Scarborough and later moved to Durham where he set up in business as a jeweller and silversmith. Out of his seven children, as far as is certain, only William and Mary developed any unusual flair for enamelling on glass.

In 1760 the family moved to Newcastle, where another brother, Ralph, an engraver of heraldic devices, was of great assistance to William and Mary Beilby in advising about the details of coats of arms and crestings. The last enamelling executed by the Beilbys was on large bucket-bowl goblets; it is beautifully detailed and shows the royal coat of arms and the signature of Beilby. Only one has been recorded bearing the initial 'W' and it is generally assumed that William and Mary shared the work between them. The first enamelled glasses by the Beilby family date from about 1762 and these show the influence of Ralph Beilby. The designs changed in about 1774 when floral motifs and miniature landscape scenes began to be painted.

The majority of Beilby glasses are decorated either with heraldic motifs in full colour or with white enamel scenes. The white enamel decorations fall into three main groups: hunting and sport scenes, landscapes showing gardens and birds, classical buildings and architectural features.

Smaller groups show masonic emblems, wine patterns, usually the simplest of their designs, and labelled decanters. Almost without exception the rims of the bowls were gilded.

There were other enamellers but these tended to be over-shadowed by the exquisite skill of the Beilbys' work. Michael Edkins, 1734-1811, was an enameller at Bristol, and used a number of skilful designs on opaque white glass. The ledgers giving facts and figures of his work have survived and have supplied useful information about the numbers of pieces which he decorated. The work of only a few other enamellers is known and their names are unrecorded.

Port decanter, enamelled by the Beilby family with Port label, vine leaves and a butterfly in white. About 1765

Other eighteenth-century table glass
Sweetmeats

Sweetmeats and champagne glasses of the eighteenth century were similar in design to the stem groups of drinking vessels, and followed the same changes in fashion. Sometimes there is even some difficulty in differentiating between the two, but it seems safe to assume that pieces with a plain edge were champagne glasses. Interesting bowl designs, including the round funnel, ogee, double ogee, and lipped double ogee, appeared. With these, the glassmaker had more scope to develop patterns and formation of bowls; the rims could be often lipped, and two well-known designs were the 'looped' and 'toothed' edges.

When early cutting was fashionable some of these sweetmeats were made with 'Van Dyke' edges, so called from the lace pattern which appeared on collars and cuffs in so many of his paintings. Scalloped edges were the alternative design to Van Dyke cutting. The majority of stems of the early period were of the simple baluster type or light baluster. The feet were domed but rarely folded. Fewer had air and opaque-twist stems.

The Silesian stem featured largely in the making of sweet-meats and champagnes with either plain or flat-cut bowls and sometimes with vertical ribbed moulded bowls. It blended well with the graceful design of these glasses. It was also used on the flat circular stands with gallery edges, made to hold small custard, jelly or syllabub glasses, one on top of the other in graduating sizes, with a sweetmeat on the top one.

During this period, important centrepieces of ingenious design were also made. Curved or 'snake'-shaped arms were joined on to the stems on which hung small-handled 'baskets', which could be passed round.

Decanters

Other table glass of the eighteenth century was made to meet the demands of the English gentry, and consisted of moulded, plain or flat-cut cream and water jugs, candle- and tapersticks, bowls, and decanters. Decanters had taken the place of the earlier dark green wine bottles, first consisting of 'cruciform' bottles (using corks), to be followed by glass-stoppered mallet- and club-shaped decanters, with engraved labels. The early faceted types of decanter and some quite plain versions, with bull's eye stoppers, date from the eighteenth century.

Punch bowl with wheel engraved floral decoration. Its cover is missing. Last quarter of 18th century

Other nineteenth-century table glass

The turn of the century brought another change in the form of the decanter. Decanters of 1800 to 1810 are usually cut with flutes and have mushroom stoppers, while during the next two decades more and more cutting of different kinds developed. The same pleasant rounded or straight-sided shapes remained. To facilitate easy handling when pouring wine into a glass, neck rings were applied separately, either one, two, three or four, sometimes plain, sometimes cut. As they were

Flute cut decanter in green glass. About 1810

cut, tiny streaks of air entered the inside surface, which occasionally discoloured the glass. These are often referred to as imperfections, but in reality they are not.

In the Victorian period the shape changed considerably and decanters became ungainly, with heavy rounded bodies and long necks and stoppers. The cutting became deeper and stoppers were made to match. Sometimes, the necks and shafts of stoppers were metal-mounted, and this was known as Sheffield plating. Modern examples tend to be made in the old patterns at most of the factories.

Ships' decanters were made with very wide bases for obvious reasons, and the best examples are quite plain with a pronounced sweep at the base, with triple- or double-ringed necks, and usually with bull's eye stoppers. Others were decorated with some sort of cutting, either flutes or diamonds.

After 1800, the fashion changed in the ornamentation of table glass, and cutting became more and more popular. There was a gradual move towards really brilliant and deep designs, covering almost the whole area of the piece. Other sorts of table glass were made in profusion. Complete sets of expensive oval and circular dishes, cruets, plates, urns and covers of many sizes, candlesticks, beautiful circular and oval fruit bowls on short stems and pedestal bases were produced.

Cut glass bowl with brilliant
diamond cutting. About 1820

Chandelier. About 1760

Lights and lighting
Candlesticks, candelabra, chandeliers

The single table candlesticks of this period used the same stem designs. Brass, pewter and silver candlesticks were already in use, also formed with knopped stems, and the glass-makers were able to draw on these designs, as well as introduce their own variations. These are now rare items, especially examples with air and opaque twist.

Contemporaneous with these were charming little taper-sticks, a smaller version of the candlestick. They were chiefly popular at tea parties, where they were placed on small tables, sometimes with brackets, to hold large tapers to light the rooms. Originally, candlesticks and tapersticks, as well as other fitments, were made with a 'saveall', small pieces of glass with a wide flange and shaft to fit into the top which was called a sconce or nozzle. These were to save the candle grease running down and could be taken out and cleaned when necessary. Few have survived the passage of time.

Only a small number were made with square bases in the faceted period. When complete examples are found, their value is increased considerably. At one time, sets of four candlesticks or tapersticks could be found from time to time, but now both pairs and singles are extremely rare. Some were decorated with rib moulding. The candelabrum was first thought of in early Georgian times and quickly became popular because it was economical as far as space on the table was concerned. The earliest surviving one is in the Victoria and Albert Museum, London, dating from about 1700. To the central column are joined four S-shaped arms with pairs and sconces. The main stem has a drop knop. The foot is domed and corrugated and the whole fitment surmounted by a moulded cone-shaped finial.

The carefully thought-out pairs of glass table candelabra produced from this period for two or more lights illustrate the ingenuity of the craftsmen. They were built up from different parts, base, arms, pans, sconces, top ornaments, and were hung with drops – the early ones being pear-shaped. To facilitate assembling, most of the parts had metal mounts.

(right) Lustre candlestick with Wedgwood decoration, candelabrum and two candlesticks. About 1735-1820

Late eighteenth-century lighting

The latter part of the eighteenth century was renowned for its great output of flat-cut table candelabra and candlesticks, wall lights, and ceiling chandeliers. Made entirely of glass, apart from the metal mounts, arm plates and chaining pins for drops, also called lustres, and the central stems, the effect of these chandeliers must have been stupendous. During the Adam era festoons of glass drops from arm to arm and urn-shaped ornaments were the main themes for candelabra. The heavy bases were either circular or square.

Wall lights were made with metal brackets to screw on the wall and with a strong metal shaft to hold them. They were on a smaller scale and included some very pleasant designs.

Regency lighting

A dramatic change took place in all these styles after 1800 to keep pace with the gaiety of Regency times. The greatest single change was that much more ormolu, or gilded bronze, appeared. Ormolu even sometimes replaced glass for the S-shaped arms, and sometimes bronze figures, usually cupids, were made on a marble base holding ormolu branches on which were fitted heavily cut pans and sconces hung with icicle drops or lustres. Icicle drops were another change from the flat-cut pear drops of the previous century. Also, long strings of 'button' drops, forming chains, extended the full length of the fitment.

Another style was to make the pan in one piece, reaching from arm to arm. These are known as 'tray top' candelabra. Instead of sconces, large hurricane shades were sometimes used. Two other types of candelabra are worthy of mention. In the first Lafont made scroll arms were fitted in two sections to join at the central plate. This was a charming style and extremely rare now. The other was known as the 'Sun Ray'. The central ornament on heavily diamond-cut candelabra was metal mounted with icicle drops of different lengths, radiating from tiny mounts, each fixed with plaster of Paris. Ormolu mounted lanterns, hanging lights and glass lace-makers' lamps formed the remainder of lighting pieces made.

Chandelier with strings of button drops and icicle drops. About 1820

English coloured glass
Bristol glass

Clear glass was manufactured at Bristol, but this has never been identified for certain. For instance, some of the rarest of all wineglasses were engraved with frigate ships and their names, Enterprise and Eagle, on the bucket-shaped bowls. These ships were based at Bristol and played an important part in England's naval history. The main coloured items produced were decanters and small bottles for sauce, all with gilt labels. Dark blue was the favourite colour, with red a close second. Green was used after about 1850.

English opaque white glass seems to have originated in Bristol where it was enamelled in colour with floral patterns, birds or little figures. Gilding was often added to accentuate details. Tea caddies, vases, candlesticks and scent bottles were produced. Michael Edkins was one of the painters at Bristol, but the decoration of the majority of the examples has now been attributed to London or south Staffordshire. It is thought that there were travelling decorators who worked in the same way as the German *Hausmaler* (see page 72).

(above) Bristol decanter in blue glass, with neck rings. About 1790

(below) Two Bristol wine-glasses. 18th century

Nailsea glass

Equally well-known is the Nailsea factory, set up in 1788 by John Robert Lucas, a cider-maker. It is known that the cheaper bottle glass was used there to make bottles and windows. In 1793, benefiting from the tax which inhibited the makers of the better quality glass, Lucas went into partnership with Edward Homer, an enamel painter, and began producing glass decorated with splashes and spots of white enamel. The Nailsea factory successfully manufactured functional glass at much lower prices than lead glass pieces.

The colour range and decoration of Nailsea glass gradually extended, with loops of different colours forming one of the commonest motifs. Items made include mugs, jugs, tumblers, jars, bottles, rolling pins and all manner of knick-knacks, such as gimmel flasks, with twin spouts, tobacco pipes, walking sticks, etc. Similar objects were made in Warrington and other places in the Midlands, which can complicate attribution. There are also a large number of Nailsea reproductions, so popular are these gay and cheerful wares. One clue to recognizing copies is that on genuine Nailsea the flecks or stripes of enamel are slightly in relief.

Dark brown sealed bottles. Extreme left and right are 17th century. centre three are 18th century

Bottle glass

Early bottles were blown with rounded bases and were supported in wicker baskets. This style continued until about 1750. Cylindrical-shaped bottles then began to develop, which eventually led to the decanter. An embossed seal was usually included on the body of bottles, carrying the coat of arms, name or cypher of the owner, and sometimes the date. This fashion lasted until the 1830s.

Collecting English glass

Naturally Ravenscroft specimens are almost wholly confined to museums. The rarest and most valuable of all are the late eighteenth-century wing-stemmed ale glasses and the heavy baluster group of glasses, dating from 1700 to 1710. Glasses which are still fairly easy to obtain are the composite stem groups, incorporating small baluster, bore and collar knops. In almost any glass sale or showrooms the remainder of the stem groups appear in profusion. Less common, however, are those with engraved bowls. Within recent years, incised,

mixed and colour-twist glasses of the mid eighteenth century have become much rarer and therefore more valuable. Sweetmeats and champagne glasses are still fairly easy to collect and there are attractive variations in both bowls and feet.

Examples of opaque white glass made at Bristol and in Staffordshire, with enamelled decoration, are now extremely rare. Blue glass decanters with gilt labels, which were reasonably common a few years ago have become more infrequent, especially signed examples. However, Stourbridge coloured glass, which is sometimes wrongly attributed to Bristol, can be collected to form an attractive group.

Cut glass dishes, bowls and decanters are available in a wide range of prices, with a simple oval diamond-cut dish at one end of the scale and a handsome Irish boat-shaped fruit bowl of about 1780 at the other. Decanters always remain obtainable.

(above) Irish decanter, with neck rings and floral decoration, from Waterloo Company, Cork. About 1800

ANGLO-IRISH GLASS

The factories

The peak of Irish glassmaking was reached in the late eighteenth century, but contrary to the usual opinion about Ireland, there were glasshouses in existence before this date. Ananias Henzey, a descendant of the Lorraine glassmaking family (see page 82) is recorded as having crossed over to Ireland from Stourbridge, and in 1668 he built a glasshouse near Portarlington, in Laoighis. Other Lorrainers were at work in Ireland at this time.

In 1780 Ireland was granted free trade and the fact that this so closely coincided in time with the English excise act, which was then burdening the glass industry in England, was instrumental in a number of glasshouses being set up in Ireland in the late eighteenth century. Many glassworkers wished to evade the heavy taxes and carry on their craft unrestricted. Deep cutting was the fashion in England in the 1780s and the Irish glassmakers of necessity followed the same styles. Irish cut glass has become famous for its quality and lustre, and in fact much cut glass of this period and design is labelled

Irish, whether the vessels originated in Ireland or not. The main centres were Dublin, Belfast, Cork and Waterford.

Not a great deal is known about glassmaking around Dublin, although three glasshouses are recorded. The first was started in 1764 by the Williams family in answer to an offer by a Dublin society to finance the 'Useful Arts'. In 1785 Charles Mulvaney set up his furnace and pieces by him are marked 'C.M. Co.' The last glasshouse is that belonging to J. D. Ayckbower, who came from London and established his works in Dublin in 1799.

In 1771 Benjamin Edwards came from Bristol to Drumrea, County Tyrone, to set up a glasshouse. In 1776 he moved to Belfast. After his death, the business was carried on by his son. The 1825 tax on glass had a damaging effect, however, and the factory closed shortly after.

The Cork Glass Company was opened in 1783 by Hayes Burnett and Rowe, and seems to have survived until 1818. The Waterloo Glass Company succeeded the Cork in 1818 and was successful until its last few years, closing in 1836.

George and William Penrose with John Hill, a glassmaker from Stourbridge, set up a Waterford factory in 1783. It continued until 1851, producing in particular flat-cut designs which like those from Bristol were often used for blue and coloured glass. The term Waterford is too widely used and it is difficult to be sure of origins of supposed Waterford glass. Nor is the greyish or blue tint associated with the name necessarily a clue as to identity.

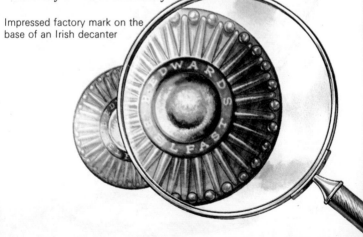

Impressed factory mark on the base of an Irish decanter

The glass

A number of factories marked their products, the name of the company or maker appearing in moulded letters with a circle on the bases of decanters, finger bowls and jugs. The lettering is often difficult to read. Marked pieces are very rare and copies have been made on which the lettering is considerably more legible.

Irish glass was suitable for cutting because, unfettered by the English taxes, heavier vessels could be made which could be cut into deep designs. The Irish craftsmen soon became noted for their skill in cutting. A vessel was first made in thick plain metal and was then marked, roughly cut, smoothed and polished. The materials used for cutting were wet sand, a sandstone wheel, a trickle of water, a fine abrasive and wheels of various sizes according to the required design.

By the early nineteenth century both simple and complex designs were in fashion, ornamenting the table glass of that time with brilliant facets, diamonds and 'steps'. The three main phases of cutting between 1770 and 1830 which affected both England and Ireland were:

1770-1800 flat geometrical and diamond designs.

Cut glass sweetmeat probably from Waterford, typical of Irish designs. About 1800

| 1800-1810 | slightly sharper diamonds and flutes in a metal of a fine dark quality, sometimes mounted with ormolu. |
| 1810-1830 | several different kinds of brilliant diamond shapes on the same piece, such as strawberry diamond, step cutting. |

The last of these was designed to create a silvery effect and was cut in deep ridges to reflect from each edge. Best known of the typical Irish pieces were the graceful flat-cut boat-shaped fruit bowls. These were usually on short knopped stems and moulded oval bases, or plain stems on small square bases. The bases were small in proportion to the size of the bowl. There were also fine oval and circular dishes, jugs, salts and other kinds of table glass.

The four main types of edge were serrated, which resembled the notches on the edge of a saw, fan-cut, which was composed of a series of flutes in a fan shape, scalloped, which was shell-shaped, and Van Dyke, which had a lacy effect (see page 104).

Collecting Irish glass
A good representative collection of Irish pieces can be gathered by the collector with only a moderate outlay. The advantage, too, of Irish cut glass is that it makes a fine display on a dining table. These vessels are functional as well as ornamental.

(right) Cut glass scent bottle. About 1820

(centre) Blue glass Irish salt cellar. About 1790

FRENCH GLASS

Stained glass windows and Nevers figures

During the Middle Ages France was famous for its production of stained and painted window glass, but it was not until the eighteenth and nineteenth centuries that other glass articles came from its factories in large quantities. In Normandy window glass was chiefly made by the crown method, while in Lorraine the broad glass process was regularly used. The crown method was older and more restricted, for it could only produce small pieces. The glass was blown, marvered and cut into round or square sections. The mark of the blowpipe always remained and gave it its name of crown. On the other hand in the broad method the glass was blown into a cylinder shape, slit lengthways and marvered, giving a sizeable and smooth sheet. Both clear and coloured window glass were produced for domestic use and for export. Glassmakers from Normandy and Lorraine carried the skill of making window glass over to England and were instrumental in founding the English glass industry.

For a long time in France very ordinary pieces were made in the Roman style. The French produced their own equivalent of the German *Waldglas*, or 'forest glass'. This was *verre de fougère*, or 'fern glass'. Although there were records of glasshouses in medieval inventories, no glass seems to have been thought valuable enough to be preserved.

Once again the style which followed was influenced by foreign glasshouses. Some of the workers who escaped from Murano came to Florence, and early pieces are almost indistinguishable from Venetian vessels of the same period. Through the marriage of an Italian prince to a French duchess, the Italian tradition was confirmed. Ludovic Gonzaga married Henrietta of Cleves and became Duke of Nevers. As a result there was an influx of glassworkers from L'Altare who settled in Nevers. In 1708 the town was called 'Le petit Muran de Venise'.

An original French style was, however, developed in this town and the most famous pieces are the little glass figures with enamelling. They are amazingly detailed, with naturalistic features, delicate lace collars and cuffs, tiny beads, buckles and walking sticks. The most popular kinds of figures were saints, rustics or actors, and occasionally huge set pieces were produced, such as the crucifixion or groups of many figures and animals in a mirror-lined case with perhaps a glass waterfall in the centre. The whole effect is colourful and exquisitely life-like.

Some of these models were particularly well-made and as they were formed from opaque glass they could be mistaken for porcelain. Probably some of a later date were direct imitations.

(left) Medallion from Nevers. 17th century. This ornament was formed from threads of coloured glass

(right) Figure of 'Winter' in opaque white glass, from Nevers. 17th century

French eighteenth- and nineteenth-century glass

Cameo-like medallions of opaque white glass decorated mugs, decanters and also rings and pendants. Desprez was one of the craftsmen who produced these attractive glass objects. French mirrors were also one of the specialities of the period. Colbert, the finance minister of Louis XIV, established a mirror-making glasshouse in Paris in order to reduce the expense of furnishing Versailles with mirrors. With the discovery of the cast glass technique which could produce sheets of glass, the new industry was able to rival Venice, until then the main manufacturer of mirrors.

The outstanding contribution of French glassmaking, however, was in the realm of *millefiori*, already used in Roman times and at Venice. Vases were made in it and other vessels, but the ideal medium was the glass paperweight. Three centres produced paperweights during the 1840s, Baccarat, Clichy and St Louis. Production reached

(below) Millefiori vase from Clichy, about 1848. These were copies of an older style

(right) French paperweight, attributed to the St Louis paperweight factory, and probably made after 1848. The decoration inside is a glass salamander

its peak during 1846 to 1849. The glasshouses were able to produce a very clear bright glass because of a source of specially pure sand.

Baccarat paperweights were often signed with a 'B', the letter referring not to the name of the factory, but to two craftsmen called Battestine who worked for the glasshouse. The date also was often included. The glass baubles covered tiny canes of many colours forming flower patterns. An innovation was introduced by the elder Battestine who began to include minute silhouettes of birds and animals, while his son incorporated a tiny elephant. Clichy paperweights sometimes show a rose, which was the sign of the factory, and some also have a 'C', St Louis weights can have small silhouettes of dancers in the design. 'S.L.' is the factory's mark, but is rare.

Varieties in the pattern are numerous, although *millefiori* form the majority, the canes either in geometrical patterns or loosely clustered. There are also coloured canes of glass on a background of *latticino* lacework, a mushroom shape of canes, imitation flowers of all kinds, realistic butterflies, snakes and reptiles. Other items with similar decoration were produced, such as hand-coolers and door handles.

Collecting French glass

Paperweights are becoming increasingly expensive. The most common is the so-called scrambled pattern, while the overlay kind is the most often imitated.

NORTH AMERICAN GLASS

Wistar and the first successful glasshouse

In 1607 a group of colonists from England settled in James-town, Virginia, and in 1608 they set up the first American glasshouse there, with the intention of exporting glass to England. The furnace was near to a forest and therefore well supplied with fuel. It seems likely that small bottles were made and perhaps beads to trade with the Indians. The venture, however, foundered, and in 1617 the glasshouse was closed. In 1621, there was a further attempt to establish the industry by some Italian glassworkers, but this also was abandoned very shortly after. Excavations have proved that glass furnaces did exist, but only fragments of glass have been found. These can give little idea of what products were made there, but they can tell us a great deal about the actual metal.

At least three other attempts were made to establish factories later in the seventeenth century in Salem, Massachusetts, and two in New Amsterdam, later to be called New York City. But no vessels survive from these works and it seems that practically all the glass used in North America during the

seventeenth and the greater part of the eighteenth century must have been imported from Europe.

In 1739 Caspar Wistar, 1696-1752, a brass button manufacturer from Philadelphia, though originating from the Netherlands, established the first successful glasshouse in Salem, New Jersey. He was not a glassmaker by trade, but a businessman with sufficient capital for the investment, and his aim was to meet the demands for everyday glass in America and to build up a profit-making concern.

Wistarberg glass was an attractive green colour and shapes were simple and functional. Decoration was usually fairly plain, involving trailing, and designed to be organically part of the whole. Wistar's workmen were skilled Dutchmen who knew the art of glassmaking and their products are of high quality. Richard Wistar, Caspar's son, carried on the business after his father's death until the glasshouse closed in 1780, but he lacked both the talent and insight of his father. The success of the Salem glasshouse led to the setting up of other furnaces, often by former employees of Wistar. In time a definite South Jersey type of glass came into being. Best known is the distinctive and attractive lily-pad pattern.

(left) Sugar bowl, possibly from Wistarberg. About 1785. The green metal is typical

(right) Mug from South Jersey. 1835-50

125

The expansion of American glassmaking

The second important establishment of a glasshouse was by
Henry William Stiegel, 1739-1785, who had formerly worked
as an ironmonger. In 1763 with the profits of this business he
set up a glasshouse at Manheim, Pennsylvania, and by 1765 he
owned three. Beginning by manufacturing bottles and window
glass, he graduated to table glass when he built his third
glasshouse. His company was renamed the American Flint
Glass Works. After a successful period of about ten years, his
business failed in 1774, mainly on account of the depression
before the American revolution, and Stiegel entered a debtor's
prison. The Stiegel glasshouses were manned by foreign
craftsmen as usual and the styles which they evolved were
partly influenced by European models and partly American
in inspiration. Decoration was enamelled, engraved and
moulded. Most original of all were the mould-blown vessels,
with a raised network pattern, known as diamond-daisy pattern and daisy-in-hexagon pattern. The metal was of a con-
sistently high standard, and colours were green, blue or
amethyst.

The third personality to interest himself in American
glassmaking in the eighteenth century was John Frederick
Amelung. Despite German financial backing and his deep

(above) Three tumblers with sulphides. 1824
(below) Engraved decanter. About 1813

personal belief that a well-managed glasshouse could be profitable on a long-term basis, as well as valuable to the country as a whole, his New Bremen glassworks did not prove to be successful in the long run and he was forced to close down in 1795. Finely engraved glass was produced, but the work was not appreciated as it deserved to be.

In Connecticut the Pitkin family had some success with their glassmaking between the years 1783 and 1831. The term 'Pitkin flask' is now widely used to describe the kind of bottle they made. The typical mode of decoration was a broken swirl design on olive-green or amber metal. The concentration was upon functional vessels.

The War of Independence, 1775-1781, inevitably dislocated the progress of the glass industry in North America, and the lack of support from the state governments did nothing to offset this. The pattern for most early glasshouses was a short period of success due to public response, but failure to establish themselves for any length of time. It was only with the invention of pressed glass that the American glasshouses really became secure.

Butter dish with Holly-
amber decoration, from
Indiana Glass Company.
1903

The invention of mechanical pressing

The first patent for the mechanical pressing of glass in
America was issued in 1825 to Bakewell's factory in Pitts-
burgh. Founded in 1808, its speciality until the development of
pressing had been lead-glass tumblers decorated with sulphides
in the bases depicting La Fayette, George Washington,
Benjamin Franklin and other outstanding men of the age. The
New England Glass Company applied for a patent in the following year and developed its own complete style of three-
mould blowing. Best known of the glasshouses to adopt
mechanical pressing, however, is the Boston and Sandwich
Glass Company, founded in 1825 by Deming Jarves, 1790-1869.
His patent was granted in 1827, and subsequently the name
'Sandwich' became synonymous with pressed glass. Jarves
invented a machine which would press out a vessel with a
handle in a single process, and this was a major advance.

The industry received a remarkable impetus from the
invention of mechanical pressing, for now not only could
cheap functional items such as tumblers be pressed in great
quantities, but the elaborate cut glass of Ireland and England

could be closely imitated at a much lower price. A number of manufacturers began to mould their names onto their glass and this often helps in identifying American pieces. The period from 1825 to 1850 has been given the title 'Lacy' because of the wealth of intricate patterns invented during the first burst of creative energy inspired by the development of pressed glass. These complex designs aimed at intensity of sparkle and had the additional advantage of disguising any flaws in the metal. After the vessel had been pressed, it was polished to give it the effect of having been cut.

As the century progressed designs became over-ambitious, with the pattern spreading out to cover the entire surface. American motifs, such as the eagle or a sheaf of wheat, were often incorporated into the more directly inspired Anglo-Irish styles. Clear glass was mainly used to begin with, but later all kinds of coloured glass were experimented with.

During the 1880s and the 1890s a vogue for exotic opaque colours and stranger shapes developed. The shades were given equally exotic names, such as peachblow (varying from rose-red to yellow) and pomona (frosted yellow glass etched with flower and fruit motifs).

Collecting American glass

Flasks and bottles decorated with the American eagle only occasionally turn up outside North America. It is possible to collect table glass representing a wide range of areas, and this is what a large number of collectors do. Pressed glass and other glassware of the 1880s are popular.

Larson bowl. 1925-35

(left) Highly decorated Victorian lustre. About 1860

(right) English Victorian table lamp. About 1860

MODERN GLASS

Victorian glass until 1851

The first years of the nineteenth century saw the continuation and further elaboration of the earlier styles of decorative glass. The glasscutters had achieved mastery of their art, and the logical development was for patterns to become more complex and to cover a greater area of the vessels. In 1845 the excise duty was removed from glass and this freed the craftsmen of England to experiment again and to compete with the rival glassmaking centres of Bohemia and North America. One new development which occurred was that of the *crystallo-ceramie*. This fashion had originated in France (see page 122) and the idea had been taken over by the owner of a London glasshouse, Apsley Pellatt, 1719-1863. Small ceramic portraits in an opaque white were covered in clear glass, and these sulphides were used to decorate small bowls, pendants, paperweights and other suitable objects d'art. George IV and other members of the royal family were numbered among his portraits. Pellatt's patent to manufacture sulphides dated from 1831, and after the repeal of the excise act there was a revival of interest in them.

Coloured glass, which was to become so popular after the

Great Exhibition of 1851, was being made earlier in the century in smaller quantities and more restrained designs. Glassmaking firms at Stourbridge, which had become the main centre for the industry in the nineteenth century and still ranks highly today, produced objects in various shades. Candlesticks with hanging glass drops became very popular and were known as lustres.

Pressed glass was, of course, introduced from America, and the first machine was bought in 1833 by W. Richardson of Stourbridge. During the following years the machines and methods extended to many other factories. The pressed glass is recognizable in its extreme geometrical precision. Fire-polishing gave brilliance to the metal, but it could not equal the brightness of cut glass. Until 1845 patterns were fairly balanced and simple, but thereafter there was a move towards more elaborate and naturalistic motifs. Floral and foliage designs became rampant. All manner of objects were pressed, tumblers, plates, salt cellars and stemmed drinking glasses, and many families could now afford copies of expensive cut glass vessels.

Overlay vase. About 1850-60.

The Great Exhibition

Henry Cole, a notable civil servant of the day, wrote of the Great Exhibition: 'The history of the World, I venture to say, records no event comparable in its promotion of human industry, with that of the Great Exhibition of the works of industry of all Nations in 1851. A great people invited all civilized nations to a festival to bring into comparison the works of human skill'. The Exhibition afforded English glassmakers an opportunity not only to display and advertise their own products, but also to see what other leading glass craftsmen of the world were producing. There is no doubt that the Exhibition, both at the time and afterwards, provided a considerable impetus to the industry.

The Crystal Palace itself, an amazing erection in sheet glass, was a monument to the technical advances of the Victorian era. The process had only been introduced into England about 1832 by Robert Chance's company, which supplied the glass for the Exhibition building. The outstanding feature inside the Exhibition was the fountain, made entirely of glass by the firm of F. and C. Osler of

Designs from the Great Exhibition

Birmingham. Standing in the central aisle, it became the focal point of the Exhibition.

After the Exhibition there was a wave of extreme styles, Egyptian, Grecian and Etruscan fashions figured, and exaggeration predominated. Coloured glass became even more popular, all manner of shades being produced, such as mazareen blue, opal chrysoprase. Opaline glass was particularly in demand, and from 1845 cased glass, in which one layer of glass was covered by a thin 'flash' of another colour, was frequently made. The satin, or matt, finish of opaque glass was developed, and simple forms were no longer sufficient. Crinkled edges, rippled trailing, stripes of colour and many combinations of colour were all employed in the continuous search for novelty.

Late Victorian glass
The Arts and Crafts Movement
The Arts and Crafts Movement was created in an attempt to bring into being a standard of well-designed and well-made furniture, glass, textiles and all the varieties of the applied arts. William Morris, 1834-1896, was the founder, a designer of international repute whose philosophy and practical work

were to have an equally important impact on future developments. Morris reacted against the cluttered patterns and over-elaboration of Victorian designs, and in 1859 he commissioned the architect and artist, Philip Webb, to design a group of wineglasses and tumblers for his own use. These were made by James Powell and Sons at the Whitefriars Glassworks in London. The glasses with their functional and simple shapes are a landmark in the history of design. When the firm of William Morris and Co. was set up more glasses were designed by Philip Webb for general sale.

The Arts and Crafts Movement was connected with the later Art Nouveau designs which developed in the majority of the countries of Europe towards the end of the century. England produced no individual glass designer to equal Emile Gallé or Louis Tiffany, although James Powell produced fine glass.

Cameo glass

A group of Stourbridge glass-makers developed a style of cameo glass during the second half of the nineteenth century which was of superb quality. Cameo scenes with classical figures, legends and motifs were produced, but there were also cameo-style vessels showing an Oriental influence, with floral and plant designs in relief. Vases, dishes and jars were made in translucent reds, pinks, blues and yellows. The overlay was always white. The most famous firm producing this glass was that set up by Thomas Webb in 1837, and he was the guiding light of the craft. Talented engravers were trained by him, including George Woodall. John Northwood, 1836-1902, was another cameo artist of note.

Collecting Victorian glass

Although the recognised date for antiques is pre-1830, later nineteenth-century glass is now becoming popular again. Certain objects are particularly sought after, such as French paperweights and ornamental lamps. Lustres have not yet really returned to favour, but in time it is possible they will.

(above) Cut overlay vase by Emile Gallé. The effect of Oriental art can be seen in the design

(left) Webb-type cameo vase with floral decoration

Art Nouveau
Emile Gallé

Emile Gallé, 1846-1904, was the outstanding exponent of Art Nouveau glass in France and many artists came to his factory to learn from him, including the American glass designer, Tiffany. Gallé's glassworks in Nancy produced ornamental glass, using the techniques of casing, tinting and relief decoration. A strong influence was the art of China and Japan, and many of his exquisite vases have raised designs of Oriental derivation. Foliage, fruit, flowers, dragonflies, all figure as delightful details on his well-formed vases. Pastel shades were his favourites, pale glowing tints, frequently blues and mauves. His glass was highly successful, and in 1889 he opened a shop in Frankfurt to sell his products.

René Lalique, 1860-1945, was close in artistic stature to Gallé, whom he studied under. Lalique started a factory in 1909 where he produced opaque glass, often in pale blue. Michael Daum, another glass designer at Nancy, was also a prominent craftsman in the Art Nouveau movement in France.

Tiffany Favrile goblet and plate

Tiffany and Favrile glass

Louis Comfort Tiffany, 1848-1933, was born into a family of jewellers in New York. He trained under the artist Emile Gallé in France and when he returned to America he set up a glasshouse in conjunction with Andrea Boldini, a Venetian glassblower. He became a leading figure in the Art Nouveau movement, which was at its height from 1880 to 1930. Apart from coloured opaque glass, he evolved Favrile glass, in which iron salt was sprayed onto the hot glass to give a metallic gloss. Tiffany's designs are always clear and flowing, the connection with plant forms and organic life being an essential aspect of Art Nouveau. Tall narrow-stemmed vases giving the impression of tulips or lilies, without slavish naturalism, are representative of his work.

Frederick Corder, 1863-1963, who emigrated from England to North America in 1903, and became manager of the Steuben glassworks there was another important figure. His teachers were the artists Fabergé, Gallé, René Lalique and Tiffany, and his art glass was in line with their designs. Corder established the quality of Steuben glass.

Lamp with fungoid decoration in style of Tiffany. About 1900

Glass of the twentieth century
Laurence Whistler

The poet, Laurence Whistler, born 1912, was the originator of the present revival of the craft of engraving on glass. He mainly uses the technique of stippling although he does also use diamond engraving. He first began by working on old goblets and rummers, as German-style *Römer* are sometimes called in England, which he had found in antique shops. But as the shapes, sizes and quality of the vessels varied so much, he began to have glasses made to his own design. These tend to be very plain, with a simple bowl, long stem and domed foot. The majority of his glasses are commissioned, and he has done work for the Steuben glasshouse in North America.

Whistler engraves his glasses with scenes, most often houses and estates. Every picture is a masterpiece, achieving an amazing contrast between light and shade. The texture varies for sky effects, foliage or details on buildings. No stippling or line engraving has been executed so expertly since David Wolff or Frans Greenwood, the Dutch artists of the eighteenth

Goblet with stippled decoration by Laurence Whistler, showing a temple being struck by lightning. The stem contains an air bubble

Vase in crystal glass engraved with a ship and seagulls by H. S. William Thomas

century. The technique has proved very popular, and its success has encouraged other artists to work in this medium. One outstanding example is the engraving by John Hutton on the great west window of Coventry Cathedral. Flying angels with trumpets are engraved with great skill, imagination and boldness.

The age of mass production

Developments in modern glass have been rapid during the early part of this century. Since the development of the first machine for pressing glass in 1825 a succession of technical leaps have been made. In 1879 the first electric light bulbs were manufactured at Corning, New York. And from then on the shades needed to screen the glare of the electric light opened up an opportunity for enterprising glassmakers. In 1915 pyrex ware, the new heat-resistant glass, was introduced to the public and the range of designs has grown rapidly since then. Fibre glass, which has been so influential in the revolutionary changes in architectural form, was developed in 1931.

Modern art glass

Not only have the great technological improvements of this century made possible the making of a greater variety of glassware for use in the home and in architecture, but also art glass has benefited from the enormous advances in techniques. Glass made for industrial purposes, plate glass used for the windows of modern skyscrapers, for transport, television and radar, would require a book on its own to render it in any detail. Therefore the concentration must be on glass vessels.

After the period of Art Nouveau when glass designers such as Emile Gallé designed not only glass but jewellery and ceramics, architects and painters turned their attention more seriously to the task of creating new forms and decorations for glass. The setting up of numerous schools of industrial design in many countries, caused by the new involvement in, and new responsibility towards, good design, has led to higher standards. Today each school specializes in one particular branch of industrial design, and this helps to ensure that design keeps pace with the techniques of this modern age.

(above) Swedish geometric-style vase, about 1950. The form is clearly connected with sculpture

(right) 'Fish Graal Vase' from Sweden. 1947

In Europe and North America, as well as the British Isles, the output of glass has continued to be on a very large scale.

In England the Stourbridge district remains famous, and there are also a number of important glasshouses around London. Scandinavian glass is perhaps the most progressive, with its emphasis on fine metal and balanced designs. Forms are strong, pure and robust, with geometrical or abstract designs being used in the main where ornament is added. The success of Scandinavian glass has been a result of the work of far-sighted design centres which maintain very high standards of workmanship.

Czechoslovakia, with the tradition of Bohemian glassmaking behind it, has revived its glass industry since the Second World War. The nationalization of the industry and the encouragement given to young artists has created the right atmosphere for new and original work. The Steuben works of North America have played an important part in modern glass development. Acting as patron for a number of internationally renowned artists, the factory has produced outstanding works of art. Steuben glass has underlined the importance of art glass as a separate branch from industrial glass.

THE TECHNIQUES OF GLASSMAKING

Chemical analysis can determine the constituents of glass, and the range of forms and shapes has been listed, but the reflective qualities of glass and its constantly changing beauty defy scientific explanation. The most remarkable fact about glass is that it is from a mixture of sand, ashes and other ingredients, all of which are themselves opaque, that objects of exceptional clarity and innumerable variety of shape can be blown simply with the aid of heat.

Constituents of glass

Glass is fundamentally made up of silica, in the form of sand, flint or quartz, heated with an alkaline flux, either potash or soda. Pure silica can be melted to form glass, but too high a temperature is required for this to be workable without the addition of an alkali. A variety of silicas have been used by different nations of glassmakers in the search for the perfect metal. The Egyptians relied on the plentiful supplies of sand which were fortunately present in their country, while the Venetians experimented with quartz-like pebbles. Seventeenth-century English workers used calcined flints which had been reduced to quicklime or powder by burning or

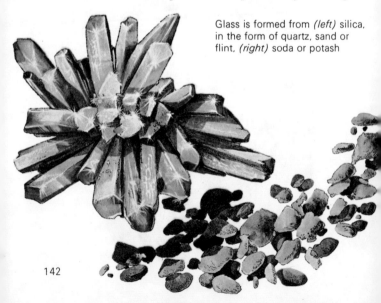

Glass is formed from *(left)* silica, in the form of quartz, sand or flint, *(right)* soda or potash

roasting. Eventually the English glassmakers found that sand was more suitable and they obtained it from coastal regions.

Careful preparation was always necessary. The sand had to be washed and the flints refined to remove brown or yellow stains which could affect the finished glass, and which sometimes can be seen on specimens. The flints were heated in a furnace until white hot and then plunged quickly into cold water which broke them into flakes suitable for calcination.

The alkaline flux has also varied according to district. The early Egyptians had an ample supply of natron, a form of soda. Soda glass which was produced in coastal areas has a lower melting point than potash glass and remains plastic longer. This quality led directly to the elaborate shapes of Mediterranean glass. Wooded areas give rise to potash glass which was heavier, and hardened at a higher temperature than soda glass. It was more suitable for the vessels decorated with cutting and engraving of Germany.

Oxide of lead introduced into the batch, the first mixing of minerals, produced a bright strong glass, famous in England after 1680. Other chemicals were also used in carefully regulated amounts and resulted in clearer softer glass being made as they prevented unwanted tints caused by impurities or chemical changes during manufacture.

Silica and the alkaline flux, when heated in a furnace, create glass. In its semi-molten state it is 'gathered' at the end of a metal rod and is ready to be blown into vessels

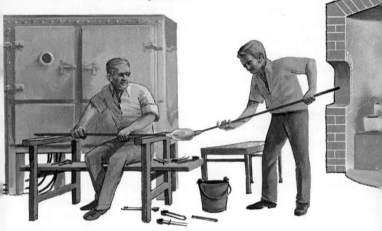

The workings of a glasshouse

The hand-made glass industry is one of the few that has remained virtually unchanged through the centuries. It is true that there are automatic and semi-automatic machines for making glass now, but this glass cannot compare with the exquisite quality of hand-made glass produced by skilled craftsmen using traditional methods and tools.

The glasshouse

The building was cone-shaped, rising to a squat chimney. The interior was simple and functional, considering the complex work which was carried out there. Inside, several circular furnaces were grouped round and joined to a central stack, each of which had a number of openings called *boccas*. These framed the mouths of crucibles in which the glass was prepared. There were several furnaces for different purposes, such as working at white heat or at a slightly lower temperature for preliminary fitting or for baking enamelled decoration.

Annealing was a process by which the molten and worked glass was cooled very gradually to normal temperature. It took place in a specially built furnace known as a *leer* or *lehr*. The process can take 24 hours and unless it is carried out correctly the glass is likely to be weakened or even to shatter.

The team of glassworkers

The scene in a glasshouse mainly consists of a group of work-men clustered around the furnace containing the pots of molten glass. A circle of workers at the furnace would gather glass from the pots and blow and work the semi-liquid metal; others would have the more leisurely job of removing articles to the annealing *lehr*. The heat from the furnaces, the noise of solid glass being knocked from used blowing irons and the light from the lumps of molten glass from the ends of irons being carried around are all part of the busy scene.

The most important work is undertaken by the 'gaffer' who sits in his special 'chair' which has wide side pieces on which he constantly rotates the heated bubble of glass white hot from the furnace. This rotary action ensures that the glass does not collapse under its own weight and helps to create a symmetrical shape.

The term 'chair' was also used to describe the small group of glassworkers who work together on any job. The gaffer is assisted by a servitor and a footmaker, as well as by an apprentice called a taker-in who carries the completed glass from the gaffer who has been working on it to the *lehr* where it will cool and harden at a strictly controlled temperature to ensure no flaws appear in the finished vessel.

Tools

The main instruments for fashioning glass in the seventeenth and eighteenth centuries were a hollow iron pipe for blowing the glass; a rod of solid iron called the pontil for handling the glass; a pair of scissors to cut the glass, also a pair of shears to cut and shape; ladles for taking the metal out of the crucibles; a hooked fork and a rake to stir the molten glass, and shovels to carry the glass about.

Glassmaking tools include scissors, shears, tongs, blow-pipe, pontil and crucible

How a glass is made

Making a wineglass is the basis of all glassmaking. A gathering of metal is first drawn on a blow-pipe by the footmaker who then blows into it, rolling it to and fro on a block of smooth iron, called a marver, to remove any irregularities from the surface and to shape the lump roughly. At this stage it is called a 'paraison'. He then blows it into a bubble of the size he wants and checks the diameter with a pair of callipers or some other gauge. The servitor adds a small blob of metal to the end of the bowl to forge the stem. This process is repeated to make the foot and this is shaped with a pair of wooden boards called clappers or palettes. A three-piece glass has now been formed, but a drawn bowl glass consists of only two pieces.

A small piece of metal is then the means of attaching a pontil to the foot, and the mouth of the wineglass is separated from the blow-pipe by touching it with a drop of water or a wetted instrument at the place where the cut is required, A sharp tap on the blow-pipe then releases the whole glass. The rough edge of the bowl is carefully trimmed with the shears and further reheating at the furnace mouth smooths it. Finally the pontil is broken off, leaving the familiar mark at the centre of the foot which is almost always present on eighteenth-century glasses.

The whole operation has to be performed with great care and skill, the glass being kept constantly in a malleable state for purposes of working. Decoration of various kinds can be added at this last stage, such as stringing, trailing or rings around the necks of decanters.

CARE AND DISPLAY OF GLASS

The display cabinet

The presentation of glass is another important aspect in collecting glass. The first requisite is a suitable display cabinet with as large an area of glass as possible in each door and with the minimum of wooden cross-pieces. It is necessary to check that the cupboard can be fitted with small electric light bulbs and efficiently wired, because this is undoubtedly the most effective way of displaying glass. If the lighting is going to be used for long periods of time it is advisable not to install too many lamps as this may lead to overheating and the danger of fire.

The shelves and background material of the cabinet should also be carefully considered. The outline of each piece of glass will vary, however slightly, and care will be needed to display each to its full advantage. To a large extent this is a matter of personal choice, but glass shelves and a background of good grey material have always been very successful.

Cleaning and repairs

Cloudiness, caused by moisture being allowed to dry on glass, can be removed by an expert, but brown wine marks in a decanter or similar vessel can be effectively eradicated by washing with vinegar, followed by a thorough rinsing. The decanter should then be dried with a number of pieces of tissue paper with the aid of a strong S-shaped metal rod until the inside is absolutely dry. Chips on the rims of bowls or stems of glasses can be polished out by an expert but this will naturally reduce the diameter as well as detract from the value of the piece. With cut glass a small chip can be effectively polished out without any harm.

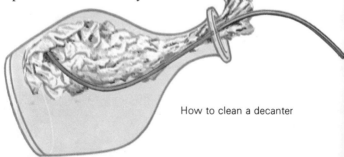

How to clean a decanter

A display cabinet showing typical pieces against a grey background

Packaging

If a glass collection or even an individual piece need to be packed for storage or for sending by post or for some other purpose, care should be taken to wrap each piece individually. First wind tissue paper around the most vulnerable part of the glass object, such as the stem or neck, and lightly pack more paper in the bowl. Wrap the whole piece in more tissue paper, then an outer layer of newspaper and place it carefully in a wooden container.

COLLECTING GLASS TODAY

Works of art of all kinds and ages are realizing high prices at the present time, and glass is becoming more sought-after every year. For those just beginning to collect glass, it is often wisest to decide on a particular period or style, such as the stem groups of the eighteenth-century English drinking glasses. There are always previews two or three days before sales and by regularly attending these, the collector will be able to assess prices and availability. Glass collecting is a very specialized subject and so it is best to specialize.

Fakes and forgeries

Care must always be taken when buying glass and it is advisable to seek the advice of a specialist. Museums are often very helpful in supplying information, and again knowledge can be gained from attending auction sales.

As in every branch of the arts, fake specimens have been produced from time to time. Very fine wineglasses have been

Jug, with folded back rim and three-reeded handle, from Turkey. 4th century AD

made in imitation of eighteenth-century glasses and these have good proportions, with the diameter of the bowl almost always less than that of the foot. An important feature to notice when checking the authenticity of early glass is the pontil mark. This occurred when a finished glass was detached from the pontil, a solid rod of iron about the same length as the blow-pipe, by a sharp tap. A rough, sometimes sharp, edge was left at the centre of the underside of the foot. Later in the eighteenth century this mark was polished out, and by 1780 the practice of grinding away the pontil mark was quite usual. It is not therefore a sure guide for glasses dating from the second half of the eighteenth century. If a genuine glass has been engraved to make it look like a valuable specimen of historical value, the engraving is usually too white or poorly defined.

These are a few hints to help the collector who is beginning a collection. Collecting glass can easily become the study of a lifetime, the more that is learnt the more there is to learn. And every fact that is learnt will help in assessing new pieces, and will contribute towards the enjoyment involved in collecting.

Dutch goblet with diamond-point engraving showing peasant revelry *façon de Venise*. The stem is winged and the foot is decorated. Late 17th century

GLOSSARY

Alkaline flux, agent, such as sodium carbonate, added to the batch to assist the materials to fuse at a workable temperature

Annealing, controlled cooling of glass to prevent strain

Annulated knop, triple-ringed knop

Batch, ingredients for making glass

Beading, decoration in the form of tiny glass droplets

Bull's eye stopper, circular stopper with 'lens' effect in centre

Close scale facet, hexagonal or diamond-shaped design in cutting

Cold painting, unfired decoration in coloured enamels

Cotton twist, decoration of thin white spirals of glass

Cruciform bottle, early bottle in shape of cross

Crizzling, fault in the form of mass of minute cracks

Cullet, broken pieces of glass, remelted to form proportion of new material, often an aid to fusing and to the final appearance of the product

Double series twist, two different types of twist used in stem, one within the other

Drawn bowl, bowl of wineglass drawn into the stem in one operation

Feathering, feather-shaped decoration made by combing

Flash, thin overlay of coloured glass on clear glass or staining

Flat cut, cutting with flat surfaces

Fluting, grooves cut in glass

Folded foot, double thickness on foot of wineglass for strength

Gadrooning, ornamental convex ridges

Gathering, blob of molten metal collected on end of blowing iron

Gimmel flask, flat glass travelling bottle

Intaglio, cut into the glass surface

Jewelling, decoration of drops of enamel

Lace twist, pattern of thin spirals of white glass

Lapidary, engraver of gems

Looped edge, applied loops on the edge of sweetmeats

Lustre, polished surface or candlestick

Marver, table of smooth iron used to remove surface irregularities on glass

Mercurial twist, type of air twist with particularly bright effect

Metal, term for glass material

Opaline, translucent opaque glass

Pedestal stem, four or more tapering moulded sides

Pillar moulding, raised ribbing by means of pincers

Pincered ornaments, decoration pinched by pincers

Plate glass, plain sheets of glass

Pontil, rough surface on centre of underside of foot where pontil rod detached

Prunt, applied decoration in the form of blobs of glass

Satin glass, smooth opaque coloured glass resembling satin

Scale pattern, trellis-moulded surface

Scrambled pattern, tiny pieces of coloured glass with no set pattern

Self-colour, monochrome

Slice-cutting, flute-cut decoration

Silver-rope twist, type of air twist

Single series twist, one type of twist used in stem

Stringing, decoration in the form of applied thin lines

Sulphide, special ceramic decoration coated with clear glass

Sweetmeat, wide-bowled vessel for sweets etc.

Tape twist, wide opaque spiral used in stem

Threading, applied lines of glass

Three-mould blowing, method of moulding in three parts

Toothed edge, cog-wheel edge on sweetmeat

Trailing, glass applied in thin bands or patterns

Two-piece glass, wineglass made in two pieces

Wrythen, moulded spiral decoration

Egyptian glassworker

Itinerant glass pedlar

19th-century glass entertainer

Important dates in the history of glassmaking

Before 3000 BC	discovery of vitreous paste
1500 BC	earliest glass vessels
500 BC	Egyptian glass industry expands
50 BC	invention of glassblowing
30 BC	conquest of Egypt by Rome
452	refugees from Aquileia settle at Venice
455	fall of Rome
622	beginning of the Mohammedan era and Islamic glass
1099	Crusaders win Jerusalem
1204	Crusaders capture Constantinople and glassworkers move to Venice
1291	Venetian glasshouses transferred to Murano
1401	Tamerlane conquers Damascus and removes glassworkers to Samarkand
1453	Turks capture Constantinople
1463	Venetian cristallo glass invented
1465	enamelling used in Venice
1575	Verzelini granted a patent to make glass in England
1608	first glasshouse established in Jamestown, Virginia
1676	Ravenscroft successfully produced glass of lead in England
1680	Bohemian crystal glass first produced
1688	cast glass made in France
1700	wheel engraving flourished in Bohemia and Silesia
1740-1780	Dutch engravers at work on English glass
1745	Glass Excise Act passed in England
1845	Glass Excise Tax repealed in England
1846-1849	peak production period for French paperweights
1825	first patent for mechanical glass pressing granted in North America
1893-1905	Louis Tiffany at work in North America

Medieval three-tier furnace

16th-century glassworkers

19th-century model of a glass engraver

English furnaces in 1700

Modern glass blower

Pressed-glass vase

BOOKS TO READ

For general introductions to the subject, the following titles are recommended and are usually available from bookshops and public libraries.

Glass Through the Ages by E. Barrington Haynes. Penguin Books, London, 1948.

Glass: a World History by F. Kämpfer and K. G. Beyer. Studio Vista, London, 1966.

The Country Life Pocket Book of Glass by Geoffrey Wills. Country Life, London, 1966.

The Country Life Book of Glass by Frank Davis. Country Life, London, 1966.

The Collector's Dictionary of Glass by E. M. Elville. Country Life, London, 1967.

The Art of Glass by W. Buckley. Allen & Unwin, London, 1939.

A Key to Pottery and Glass by B. Rackham, Blackie & Sons, London, 1940.

Ancient Glass by F. Neuburg. Translated by M. Bullock. Barrie & Rockliffe, London, 1962.

Old Venetian Glass by K. Hettěs. Translated by O. Vojtíšek, Spring Books, London, 1960.

History of Old English Glass by Francis Buckley. Ernest Benn, London, 1925.

Old English Drinking Glasses by G. R. Francis. Herbert Jenkins, London, 1926.

A History of English and Irish Glass in 2 volumes by W. A. Thorpe. Medici Society, London, 1929.

English Table Glass by E. M. Elville. Country Life, London, 1951.

English and Irish Cut Glass by E. M. Elville. Country Life, London, 1954.

Coloured Glass by Derek Davis and Keith Middlemas. Herbert Jenkins, London, 1968.

Paper Weights and Other Glass Curiosities by E. M. Elville. Country Life, London, 1954.

Places to visit

The British Museum, London, S.W.7.
Pilkington Glass Museum, St Helens, Lancashire.
The Victoria and Albert Museum, South Kensington, London, S.W.7.
The Corning Museum of Glass, New York, U.S.A.

INDEX

Page numbers in **bold** type refer to illustrations.

SOME OTHER TITLES IN THIS SERIES